MW01273269

Scale	8 1/2 × 11	11 × 17						
1" = 10'	85 × 110	110 × 170	170 × 220	180 × 240	220 × 340	240 × 360	300 × 420	360 × 480
1" = 20'	170 × 220	220 × 340	340 × 440	360 × 480	440 × 680	480 × 720	600 × 840	720 × 960
1" = 30'	255 × 330	330 × 510	510 × 660	540 × 720	660 × 1020	720 × 1080	900 × 1260	1080 × 1440
1" = 40'	340 × 440	440 × 680	680 × 880	720 × 960	880 × 1360	960 × 1440	1200 × 1680	1440 × 1920
1" = 50'	425 × 550	558 × 850	850 × 1100	900 × 1200	1100 × 1700	1200 × 1800	1500 × 2100	1800 × 2400
1" = 60'	510 × 660	660 × 1020	1020 × 1320	1080 × 1440	1320 × 2040	1440 × 2160	1800 × 2520	2160 × 2880
3" = 1'-0"	2.83 × 3.67	3.67 × 5.67	5.67 × 7.34	6 × 8	7.33 × 11.34	8 × 12	10 × 14	12 × 16
1 1/2" = 1'-0"	5.67 × 7.34	7.34 × 11.34	11.34 × 14.67	12 × 16	14.67 × 22.67	16 × 24	20 × 28	24 × 32
1" = 1'-0"	8.5 × 11	11 × 17	17 × 22	18 × 24	22 × 34	24 × 36	30 × 42	36 × 48
3/4" = 1'-0"	11.33 × 14.66	14.67 × 22.67	22.67 × 29.34	24 × 32	29.34 × 45.34	32 × 48	40 × 56	48 × 64
1/2" = 1'-0"	17 × 22	22 × 34	34 × 44	36 × 48	44 × 68	48 × 72	60 × 84	72 × 96
1/4" = 1'-0"	34 × 44	44 × 68	68 × 88	72 × 96	88 × 136	96 × 144	120 × 168	144 × 192
1/8" = 1'-0"	68 × 88	88 × 136	136 × 176	144 × 192	176 × 272	192 × 288	190 × 336	288 × 384
1/16" = 1'-0"	136 × 176	176 × 272	272 × 352	288 × 384	352 × 544	384 × 576	480 × 672	576 × 768

Sheet size in the drawing editor according to the scale of drawings and final plotted sheet sizes

Measurement System	AutoCAD's Display of Measurement	
Scientific	1.55E + 01	(inches)
Decimal	15.5000	(inches)
Engineering	1'-3.5"	(input as 1'3.5")
Architectural	1'-3 1/2"	(input as 1'3-1/2")
Metric	15.5000	(converted to metric at plot)
Fractional	15 1/2"	(input as 15-1/2")

Measurement systems available in AutoCAD

Drawing Scale	Scale Factor	AutoCAD Drawing Height for 1/8"-High Text
1/16" = 1'-0"	192	24.0"
1/8" = 1'-0"	96	12.0"
1/4" = 1'-0"	48	6.0"
1/2" = 1'-0"	24	3.0"
3/4" = 1'-0"	16	2.0"
1" = 1'-0"	12	1.5"
1 1/2" = 1'-0"	8	1.0"
3" = 1'-0"	4	0.5"

1/8-inch-high text converted to size for various drawing scales

Computer users are not all alike.
Neither are SYBEX books.

We know our customers have a variety of needs. They've told us so. And because we've listened, we've developed several distinct types of books to meet the needs of each of our customers. What are you looking for in computer help?

If you're looking for the basics, try the **ABC's** series, or for a more visual approach, select **Teach Yourself**.

Mastering and **Understanding** titles offer you a step-by-step introduction, plus an in-depth examination of intermediate-level features, to use as you progress.

Our **Up & Running** series is designed for computer-literate consumers who want a no-nonsense overview of new programs. Just 20 basic lessons, and you're on your way.

SYBEX **Encyclopedias** provide a *comprehensive reference* and explanation of all of the commands, features and functions of the subject software.

Sometimes a subject requires a special treatment that our standard series doesn't provide. So you'll find we have titles like **Advanced Techniques, Handbooks, Tips & Tricks**, and others that are specifically tailored to satisfy a unique need.

You'll find SYBEX publishes a variety of books on every popular software package. Looking for computer help? Help Yourself to SYBEX.

For a complete catalog of our publications:

SYBEX Inc.

2021 Challenger Drive, Alameda, CA 94501

Tel: (415) 523-8233/(800) 227-2346 Telex: 336311

Fax: (415) 523-2373

SYBEX is committed to using natural resources wisely to preserve and improve our environment. This is why we have been printing the text of books like this one on recycled paper since 1982.

This year our use of recycled paper will result in the saving of more than 15,300 trees. We will lower air pollution effluents by 54,000 pounds, save 6,300,000 gallons of water, and reduce landfill by 2,700 cubic yards.

In choosing a SYBEX book you are not only making a choice for the best in skills and information, you are also choosing to enhance the quality of life for all of us.

AutoCAD
Release 11
Instant Reference

AutoCAD®
Release 11
Instant Reference
Second Edition

George Omura

SYBEX®

San Francisco · Paris · Düsseldorf ·Soest

Acquisitions Editor: Dianne King
Developmental Editor: James A. Compton
Copy Editor: Jim Miller
Project Editor: Janna Hecker
Technical Editor: Frank Ashford
Assistant Editor: Barbara Dahl
Word Processors: Scott Campbell and Ann Dunn
Book Designer: Ingrid Owen
Production Artist: Helen Bruno
Screen Graphics: Cuong Le
Typesetter: Deborah Maizels
Proofreader: Lisa Haden
Indexer: Tom McFadden
Cover Designer: Archer Design
Screen reproductions produced by XenoFont.

Library of Congress Card Number: 91-65511
ISBN: 0-89588-732-0

Manufactured in the United States of America
10 9 8 7 6 5 4 3 2 1

To my son, Arthur

Acknowledgments

Book projects such as this require a team effort. My thanks and appreciation go to the many people at SYBEX who made the AutoCAD Instant Reference possible, particularly the following: Dianne King, who got things started; Jim Compton, who kept me on track; Jim Miller, who clarified points large and small; Frank Ashford, who made many valuable suggestions throughout; and Janna Hecker, who kept all the pieces together.

Copyeditor Deborah Craig and technical reviewer Ken Morgan made significant contributions to the previous edition of this book, and much of their work is incorporated here.

At Autodesk, Inc., Patricia Peper and Gloria Bastidas were invaluable in furnishing current software.

Table of Contents

Introduction

This book is designed to give you quick and comprehensive answers to your AutoCAD questions. Whether you are stymied by a function or command that does not work as you intended or just want a quick refresher on a procedure, *AutoCAD Instant Reference* will help you solve the problem quickly so you can get on with your work. All of AutoCAD's many features are here—the basic commands as well as the built-in functions you may not use every day. All information is current for AutoCAD through release 11. Each entry notes the earliest version in which the feature being discussed is available.

WHO SHOULD USE THIS BOOK

AutoCAD Instant Reference is designed for users who have some familiarity with AutoCAD—who have an idea of what they need to know but aren't quite sure how all of AutoCAD's features work. It is equally useful for casual AutoCAD users who need basic information fast and experienced users who need a refresher on a certain command.

If you are new to AutoCAD and want a tutorial format, you can read my *Mastering AutoCAD* (Sybex, 4th edition 1991), which contains a wealth of tips and techniques for both beginning and advanced users. *AutoCAD Instant Reference* is an excellent companion to *Mastering AutoCAD*, providing concise descriptions of every AutoCAD command and its advanced features.

HOW THIS BOOK IS ORGANIZED

The entries for individual AutoCAD commands appear in alphabetical order. Each entry presents the following information:

- The AutoCAD versions in which the command is available. Where items vary between versions, the version number is shown in parentheses next to the item.

- A brief statement of the command's purpose.

- The sequence of steps you use to invoke the command and to provide AutoCAD with necessary information.

- Notes describing restrictions explaining interactions with other commands, and providing special tips or warnings.

- A list of related entries to consult for further information.

Options from the AutoCAD opening main menu are listed by name. In cases where main menu options duplicate commands, such as Plot and Files, the option is described under the command name.

AutoCAD Instant Reference also describes many of the AutoCAD utilities and support files, such as Cfig386.EXE for memory management and Slidelib.EXE for creating slide libraries.

Commands

ACAD.PGP

● **VERSIONS**   2.1 and later. Version 11 adds command alias.

● **PURPOSE**   An ASCII file that contains information needed to launch a DOS program from within AutoCAD. Acad.pgp is also where command alias definitions are located. Most of the commands in the Utility-External Commands menu need this file.

To Edit the Acad.pgp File

You can edit Acad.pgp using any word processor that will save files in the ASCII format. Figure 1 gives a partial listing of this file.

● **NOTES**   In the external command section, the first item in each entry is the command name to be entered at the AutoCAD command prompt. The second item is the actual command as entered at the DOS prompt. Next is the amount of memory in bytes to allocate to the command. Usually, 30K is enough memory for DOS functions. The maximum allowable ranges from 320K to 400K. The fourth item specifies the prompt, if there is any, that appears after the command is issued. An asterisk preceding the prompt tells AutoCAD to accept spaces in the response to the prompt. The response is appended to the prompt. If no prompt is needed, this item can be blank. The last item is a return code, usually 0. Other return codes are:

1 = Load the file $cmd.DXB when the command is terminated.

2 = Create a block with the name from the prompt. Block entities will be taken from the file $cmd.DXB. This return code must be used in conjunction with the 1 code.

4 = Restore the previous screen mode (text or graphics).

The command alias format is simple. The first item is the alias. It is followed by a comma, a space, and the name of the command being aliased. An asterisk prefixes the command name.

See Also   Commands: Alias, Catalog, Del, Dir, Edit, Shell, Shroom.COM, Type

```
; acad.pgp - External Command and Command Alias definitions

; External Command format:
;   <Command name>,[<DOS request>],<Memory reserve>,[*]<Prompt>,<Return code>

; Examples of External Commands for DOS

CATALOG,DIR /W,33000,File specification: ,0
DEL,DEL,      33000,File to delete: ,0
DIR,DIR,      33000,File specification: ,0
EDIT,EDLIN,   42000,File to edit: ,0
SH,,          33000,*OS Command: ,0
SHELL,,       127000,*OS Command: ,0
TYPE,TYPE,    33000,File to list: ,0

; Command alias format:
;   <Alias>,*<Full command name>

; Sample aliases for AutoCAD Commands
; These examples reflect the most frequently used commands.
; Each alias uses a small amount of memory, so don't go
; overboard on systems with tight memory.

A,     *ARC
C,     *CIRCLE
```

Figure 1: External command and command alias definitions

ALIAS
(AUTOLISP)

● **VERSIONS**   11

● **PURPOSE**   Displays the command aliases stored in the Acad.pgp file. Command aliases are abbreviations of command names that simplify keyboard access to commands.

To Select the Alias Command

- From the keyboard: (**load "<drive>:/path/alias"**)⏎**alias**⏎

- From the screen menu: **Bonus-Alias**

● **NOTES**   From the keyboard, you have to load Alias only once per editing session. You can then use Alias at any time. It is not necessary to load Alias if you are using the menu.

See Also   AutoLISP

ALIGNED (DIM)

● **VERSIONS**   2.0 and later

● **PURPOSE**   Aligns a dimension with two points or an object. The dimension text appears in the current text style. Figure 2 illustrates the difference between aligned and rotated dimensions.

Before Dimensioning

You must have issued the Dim or Dim1 command to use any dimensioning subcommand.

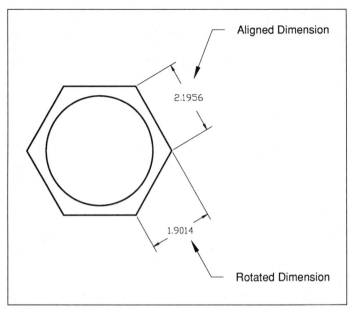

Figure 2: Aligned and rotated dimensions

To Align a Dimension

- From the keyboard: **Aligned** ↵

- From the screen menu: **Dim-Linear-Aligned**

Then follow these steps:

1. **First extension line origin or RETURN to select:** Pick one end of object or an entire line arc, or circle to be dimensioned.

2. **Second extension line origin:** Pick other end of the object. This prompt does not appear for objects.

3. **Dimension line location:** Pick a point or enter coordinate for the location of the dimension line.

4. **Dimension text: <default dimension>:** Press ↵ to accept the default dimension or enter dimension value.

5. The dimension aligns with the two points you selected at the **extension line** prompts. If you selected line, arc, or circle, the dimension is aligned with the object.

ANGULAR (DIM)

● **VERSIONS**   2.0 and later

● **PURPOSE**   Creates a dimension label showing the angle described by an arc, circle, two lines, or by a set of three points. An arc with dimension arrows at each end is drawn and the angle value is placed using the current text style.

Before Dimensioning

You must have issued the Dim or Dim1 command to use any dimensioning subcommand.

To Create an Angle Dimension Label

• From the keyboard: **Angular ↵**

• From the screen menu: **Dim-Angular**

Then follow these steps:

1. **Select arc, circle, line, or RETURN:** Pick an object as indicated by the prompt or press ↵ to indicate angles using your cursor.

2. If you pressed ↵, continue with step 4. If you selected an arc or circle, skip to step 7. If you selected a line, the prompt **Second line:** appears. After picking a second line, continue at step 7.

3. **Angle vertex:** Pick a point indicating the center angle vertex.

4. **First angle endpoint:** Pick a point indicating the first angle.

5. **Second angle endpoint:** Pick a point indicating the second angle.

6. **Enter dimension line arc location:** Pick a point indicating the location of the dimension line arc.

7. **Dimension text <default dimension>:** Press ↵ to accept default angle or enter angle value.

8. **Enter text location:** Pick the location for the beginning of the dimension text.

In versions 10 and earlier, the following two steps replace steps 2 through 6:

1. **Select first line:** Pick one of two lines for the angular dimension.

2. **Second line:** Pick the other line for the angular dimension.

● **NOTES** At the **Dimension text** prompt, you can append text to the default dimension value. See Appending Dimension Text.

APERTURE

● **VERSIONS** 2.0 and later

● **PURPOSE** Sets the size of the Osnap (object snap) target box to your preference.

Sequence of Steps

• From the keyboard: **Aperture**↵

- From the screen menu: **Settings-Aperture**

Then complete the following step:

Object snap target height (1-50 pixels) <5>: Enter desired size of Osnap target in pixels.

Default settings may vary depending on your display.

See Also   Commands: Osnap, Osnap overrides. System Variables: Aperture

APPENDING DIMENSION TEXT (DIM)

- **VERSIONS**   2.5 and later

- **PURPOSE**   At the **Dimension text** prompt, you can append text to the default dimension text.

Before Dimensioning

You must have issued the Dim or Dim1 command to use any dimensioning subcommand.

To Enter Dimension Text

- At the prompt **Dimension text <text>:** place <> signs where you want text to appear, then enter the text.

See Also   Dimension Variables: Dimapost, Dimpost

ARC

- **VERSIONS**   All versions

- **PURPOSE**   Allows you to draw an arc using a variety of methods.

To Draw an Arc

- From the keyboard: **Arc**↵

- From the screen menu: **Draw-Arc**

- From the pull-down menu: **Draw-Arc**

Then complete the following step:

Center/<Start point>: C or use the mouse to pick the start point of the arc.

If you select Arc from the screen menu, the arc menu appears, with several preset Arc options. Figure 3 illustrates how these options draw arcs.

- **OPTIONS**

Angle   Enters an arc in terms of degrees or current angular units. You are prompted for the **Included angle**. You can enter an angle value or use the cursor to visually select an angle.

Center   Enters the location of an arc's center point. At the prompt **Center**, enter a coordinate or pick a point with your cursor.

Direction   Enters a tangent direction from the start point of an arc. At the prompt **Direction from start point** either enter a relative coordinate or pick a point with your cursor.

End   Enters the end point of an arc. At the prompt **End point**, enter a coordinate or pick a point with your cursor.

Length   Enters the length of an arc's chord. At the prompt **Length of chord**, enter a length or pick a length with your cursor.

Radius   Enters an arc's radius. At the prompt **Radius**, enter a radius or pick a point that defines a radius length.

Start point   Enters the beginning point of an arc.

● NOTES   If you press ⏎ at the first prompt of the Arc command, AutoCAD uses the most recent point entered for a line or arc as the first point of the new arc. It then prompts you for a new end point. An arc is drawn tangent to the last line or arc drawn.

The Arc screen menu provides several predefined Arc option sequences. For example, S,E,D allows you to select the start point, the end point, and the direction of the arc.

You can convert arcs to polyline arcs with the Pedit command.

See Also   Commands: Change/Thickness, Elev, UCS

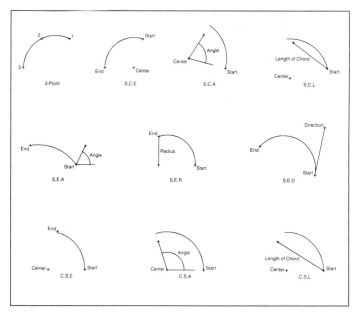

Figure 3: The Arc menu options and their meanings

AREA

- **VERSIONS**   All versions

- **PURPOSE**   Carries out an area calculation based on dimensions that you specify by defining line segments, by selecting lines and polylines, or both.

Sequence of Steps

- From the keyboard: **Area** ↵

- From the screen menu: **Inquiry-Area**

- From the pull-down menu: **Utility-Area** (11)

Then follow these steps:

1.   **<First point>/Entity/Add/Subtract:** Pick the first point or enter the option.

2.   Each time you select a point the following prompt appears:

   Next Point:

   Pick the next point. Continue picking points until you have defined the area, then press ↵.

- **OPTIONS**

Next point   Continues selecting points until you have defined the area to be calculated. Once you have defined the area, press ↵ at the **Next point** prompt.

Entity   Selects a circle or polyline for area calculation. If you pick an open polyline, AutoCAD will calculate the area of the polyline as if its two end points were closed.

Add   Keeps a running count of areas. Normally, Area returns you to the **Command** prompt as soon as an area has been calculated. If you enter the Add mode, once an area has been calculated, you are returned to the **Areas** command prompt and you can continue to add area values to the current area.

Subtract   Subtracts areas from a running count of areas.

● **NOTES**   Area does not calculate areas for arcs. To find the area of a shape that includes arcs, convert the arc areas into polylines (see Pedit) before you issue the Area command. Select the Entity option and pick the polyline. Area calculates the area of the polyline. Add the polyline areas to rectangular areas to arrive at the total area.

Area only calculates areas in a plane parallel to the current User Coordinate System.

See Also   Commands: Dblist, List. System Variables: Area

ARRAY

● **VERSIONS**   All versions

● **PURPOSE**   Makes multiple copies of an object or group of objects in a row-and-column matrix, a single row or column, or a circular array (to form such objects as teeth in a gear or the numbers on a circular clock).

To Create Object Arrays

●   From the keyboard: **Array.**↵

●   From the screen menu: **Edit-Array**

●   From the pull-down menu: **Modify-2D Array** (11)

Then follow these steps:

1.   **Select objects:** Pick objects to array.

2.   **Rectangular or Polar array (R/P):** Enter the desired array type.

If you enter **R** at the **Rectangular or Polar** prompt, you are given the following series of prompts:

   3.   **number of rows (---) <1>:** Enter the number of rows.

   4.   **number of columns (I I I) <1>:** Enter the number of columns.

   5.   **Unit cell or distance between rows (---):** Enter the depth of the cell.

If you enter **P** at the **Rectangular or Polar** prompt, you are given the following prompts:

   6.   **Center point of array:** Pick the center of rotation.

   7.   **Number of items:** Enter the number of items in the array, including the originally selected objects.

   8.   **Angle to fill <360>:** Enter the angle the array is to occupy. Use a negative value to indicate a clockwise array.

   9.   **Rotate objects as they are copied? <Y>:** Enter **N** if the arrayed objects are to maintain their current orientation.

● OPTIONS

Rectangular   Copies the selected objects in the array of rows and columns. You are then prompted for the number of and distance between the rows and columns.

Polar   Copies the selected objects in a circular array. You are prompted first for the center point of the array and then for the number of items in the array. You are asked whether you want to rotate the objects as they are copied. If you press ↵ without entering a value at the **Number of items** prompt, you will be prompted for the angle between items.

Center   Entering **Center** or **C** at the **Rectangular** or **Polar** prompt allows you to enter the center point of a polar array. You are prompted for the angle between items and the number of items or degrees to fill. You are asked whether you want the objects to be rotated as they are copied.

• **NOTES**   Usually, row and column arrays are aligned with the X and Y axes of your current user coordinate system. To create an array at any other angle, set the Snap command's Rotate option to the desired angle. Rectangular arrays will be rotated by the snap angle (see Figure 4). The Snapang system variable also allows you to set the cursor rotation angle.

See Also   Commands: Minsert, Select, Snap/Rotate. System Variables: Snapang

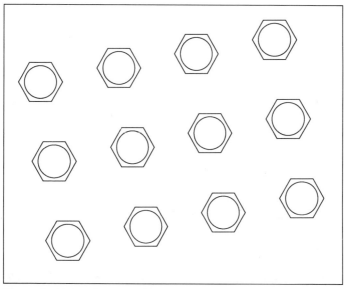

Figure 4: Rotated rectangular array

ASCTEXT (AUTOLISP)

• **VERSIONS**   10, 11

● **PURPOSE** Imports ASCII text files into your drawing. Asctext has options with which you can control the text's appearance, such as underlining, line spacing, and columns.

To Import a Text File Using Asctext

- From the keyboard: **(load "<drive>:/path/asctext")**↵
  Asctext↵

- From the screen menu: **Bonus-Asctext** (11)

Then follow these steps:

1. **File to read (including extension):** Enter the ASCII file name.

2. **Start point or Center/Middle/Right:** Pick the start point or enter **C, M,** or **R** for the desired option.

3. **Height: <default>:** Enter the height.

4. **Rotation angle:** Enter the angle.

5. **Change text options? <N>:** Enter **Y** to specify text insertion options or press ↵ to import text.

If you enter **Y** at the **Change text options** prompt, you will get the following series of prompts:

6. **Distance between lines/<Auto>:** Enter a distance or press ↵ to accept the default.

7. **First line to read/<1>:** Enter the number of the first line to be read from the ASCII file.

8. **Number of lines to read/<A11>:** Enter the number of lines to be read from the ASCII file.

9. **Underscore each line? <N>:** Enter **Y** to underscore each line.

10. **Overscore each line? <N>:** Enter **Y** to overscore each line.

11. **Change text case? Upper/Lower/<N>:** Enter **U** to change all the text read from the ASCII file to upper-case, **L** to change to lowercase, or ↲ for no change.

12. **Set up columns? <N>:** Enter **Y** to set up multiple columns of text or ↲ to begin importing the file.

If you enter **Y** at the **Set up columns** prompt, the following prompts appear:

13. **Distance between columns:** Enter the distance.

14. **Number of lines per column:** Enter the number of lines.

● **NOTES**   When you specify a file name at the **File to read** prompt, use the forward slash (/) rather than the backslash (\) when specifying directories. You can also use the double backslash (\\).

From the keyboard, you only have to load Asctext once per editing session. You can then use Asctext at any time. It is not necessary to load Asctext if you are using the menu.

See Also   AutoLISP

ATTDEF

● **VERSIONS**   1.4 and later

● **PURPOSE**   Creates an attribute definition that allows you to store textual and numeric data with a block. When you insert a block containing an attribute definition into a drawing, you are prompted for the data that is to be stored with the block. Later, you can use the Ddatte or List command to view the data, or use the Attext command to extract it into an ASCII text file. You can control the format of the extracted file for easy importation to database manager, spreadsheet, or word processing programs.

To Create an Attribute Definition with Attdef

- From the keyboard: **Attdef**↵

- From the screen menu: **Blocks-Attdef**

Then follow these steps:

1. **Attribute modes—Invisible:N Constant:N Verify:N Preset:N Enter (ICVP) to change, RETURN when done:** Enter **I**, **C**, **V**, or **P** to toggle an option on or off, or press ↵ to go to the next prompt.

2. **Attribute tag:** Enter the attribute name.

3. **Attribute prompt:** Enter the prompt to be displayed for attribute input.

4. **Default attribute value:** Enter the default value for attribute input.

5. **Justify/Style/<Start point>:** Enter coordinates with the cursor to select the location of attribute text, or select an option to determine orientation or style of the attribute text.

6. **Height (2.000.:** Enter the attribute text height and press ↵. Prompt appears only if the current text style height is set to 0.

7. **Rotation angle <0>:** Enter the angle of the attribute text ↵.

● OPTIONS

Invisible Makes the attribute invisible when inserted.

Constant Gives the attribute a value that you cannot change.

Verify Allows review of the attribute value after insertion.

Preset Automatically inputs the default attribute value on insertion. Unlike the Constant option, it lets you change the input value of a preset attribute by using the Ddatte or Attedit commands. See Text for Attdef options related to location, style, and orientation of attributes.

See Also   Commands: Attdisp, Attedit, Attext, Block, Ddatte, Insert, Text, Xdata/Xdlist. System Variables: Aflags, Attdia, Attreq

ATTDISP

● **VERSIONS**   All versions

● **PURPOSE**   Allows you to control the display and plotting of all attributes in a drawing. You can force attributes to be displayed according to their display mode, or made invisible.

To Set Attribute Display Using Attdisp

● From the keyboard: **Attdisp.⏎**

● From the screen menu: **Blocks-Attdisp**

Then complete the following step:

Normal/ON/OFF <Normal>: Enter **ON**, **OFF**, or ⏎ for your selection.

● **OPTIONS**

Normal   Hides attributes that are set to be invisible. All other attributes are displayed.

ON   Displays all attributes, including those set to be invisible.

OFF   Hides all attributes, whether or not they are set to be invisible.

● **NOTES**   If autoregeneration is on (see Regenauto), your drawing will regenerate when you complete the command, and the display of attributes will reflect the option you select. If autoregeneration is off, the drawing will not regenerate until you issue Regen.

See Also   Commands: Attdef, Regen, Regenauto. System Variables: Aflags, Attmode

ATTEDIT

● **VERSIONS**   All versions

● **PURPOSE**   Edits attribute values after you have inserted them in a drawing. You can edit attributes individually or globally.

To Edit Attribute Values with Attedit

- From the keyboard: **Attedit ↵**
- From the screen menu: **Edit-Attedit**

Then follow these steps:

1. **Edit attributes one at a time? <Y>:** Enter **Y** for individual or **N** for global attribute editing.

A different prompt may appear, depending on whether you enter Y or N. The following prompts always appear:

2. **Block name specification <*>:** Enter the block name to restrict the attribute edits to a specific block, or enter a wildcard filter list.

3. **Attribute tag specification <*>:** Enter an attribute tag to restrict attribute edits to a specific attribute, or enter the wildcard filter list.

4. **Attribute value specification <*>:** Enter a value to restrict attribute edits to a specific attribute value, or enter the wildcard filter list.

In most cases, the next prompt asks you to select an attribute. Pick the attributes you want to edit. If you elected to edit the attributes

one at a time, an **X** appears on the first attribute to be edited, and
you will see the prompt:

5.   **Value/Position/Height/Angle/Style/Layer/Color/
Next/<N>:** Select an option.

• OPTIONS

Y (at first prompt)   Allows you to edit attribute values one at a
time, and change an attribute's position, height, angle, text style,
layer, and color.

N (at first prompt)   Allows you to globally modify attribute
values. If you select this option, you are asked whether you want to
edit only visible attributes .

Value   Changes the value of the currently marked attribute(s).

Position   Moves an attribute.

Height   Changes the height of attribute text.

Angle   Changes the attribute angle.

Style   Changes the attribute text style.

Layer   Changes the layer that the attribute is on.

Color   Changes the attribute color. Colors are specified by
numeric code or by name. See Color.

• NOTES   If you choose to edit attributes individually and
answer all of the prompts (you selected Y at the first prompt), you
are prompted to select attributes. After you have made your selection, an **X** marks the first attribute to edit. The default option, Next,
will move the marking **X** to the next attribute.

By entering **V** at the **Value/Position/Height** prompt, you can
proceed to either change or replace the attribute value. If you
choose Replace, the default option, you are prompted for a new attribute value. The new attribute value replaces the previous one
and you return to the **Value/Position/Height** prompt. If you
choose Change, you are prompted for a specific string of characters
to change and for a new string to replace the old. This allows you to

change portions of an attribute's value without having to enter the entire attribute value.

If you choose to edit only visible attributes (after entering N at the first prompt), you are prompted to select attributes. You can then visually pick the attributes to edit. You are next prompted for the string to change and the replacement string. Once you have answered the prompts, AutoCAD changes all the selected attributes. If you enter **N** at the **Visible attribute** prompt, you won't be prompted to select attributes. Instead, AutoCAD assumes you want to edit all the attributes in the drawing, whether or not they are visible. The **Select attribute** prompt is skipped and you are sent directly to the **Change string** prompt.

When answering the attribute specification prompts, you can use wildcard characters (the question mark and the asterisk) to "filter" a group of attribute blocks, tags, or values.

To restrict attribute edits to attributes that have a null value, enter a backslash (\) at the attribute value specification prompt.

See Also   Commands: Ddatte, Select, Wildcards

ATTEXT

● **VERSIONS**   All versions

● **PURPOSE**   Converts attribute information into external ASCII text files. You can then bring these files into database or spreadsheet programs for analysis. Attext allows you to choose from three standard database and spreadsheet file formats.

To Make an Attext Conversion

- From the keyboard: **Attext↵**
- From the screen menu: **Utility-Attext**

Then follow these steps:

1. **CDF, SDF or DXF Attribute extract (or Entities)? <C>:**
Enter the format of the extracted file or ↵ to select specific attributes for extraction.

In version 11, the files dialog box appears. Earlier versions display the **Template file:** prompt. Enter the name of the external template file.

2. Once a template file is selected, the next prompt appears:

Extract file name <drawing name>:

Enter the name of the file to hold the extracted information.

● OPTIONS

CDF (comma delimited file) Creates an ASCII file using commas to delimit fields. Each attribute is treated as a field of a record, and all the attributes in a block are treated as one record. Character fields are enclosed in quotes. Some database programs such as dBASE III, III PLUS, and IV can read this format without any alteration.

SDF (space delimited format) Creates an ASCII file using spaces to delimit fields. Each attribute is treated as a field of a record, and all attributes in a block are treated as one record. The field values are given a fixed width, and character fields are not given special treatment. If you open this file using a word processor, the attribute values appear as rows and columns (the rows are the records and the columns are the fields).

DXF (data exchange format) Creates an abbreviated AutoCAD DXF file that contains only the block reference, attribute, and end of sequence entities. **Entities** prompts you to select objects. You can then select specific attributes to extract. Once you are done with the selection, the **Attribute extract** prompt reappears.

● **NOTES** Before you can extract attribute values with Attext, you need to create a *template* file, an external ASCII file containing a list of attribute tags you wish to extract. Template files, which have the extension .TXT, also contain a code describing the characteristics of the attribute associated with the tag. The code denotes character and numeric values as well as the number of characters for string values or the number of placeholders for numeric values. For example, if you expect the value entered for a numeric attribute whose tag is *cost* to be five characters long with two decimal places, include the following line in the template file:

cost   N005002

The **N** indicates that this attribute is a numeric value. The next three characters indicate the number of digits the value will hold. The last three characters indicate the number of decimal places the number will require. If you want to extract a character attribute, you might include the following line in the template file:

name   C030000

The **C** denotes a character value. The next three characters indicate the number of characters you expect for the attribute value. The last three characters in character attributes are always zeroes, because character values have no decimal places.

Follow the last line in the template file by a ↵, or you will receive an error message when you try to use the template file.

You can also extract information about the block that contains the attributes. Table 1 shows the format you use in the template file to extract block information. A template file containing these codes must also contain at least one attribute tag, because AutoCAD must know which attribute it is extracting before it can tell what block the attribute is associated with.

See Also   Commands: Attdef, Attedit. System Variables: Fildia

ATTREDEF (AUTOLISP)

● **VERSIONS**   9 and later

● **PURPOSE**   Redefines a block that contains attributes. Attredef automatically updates the location, angle, and style of existing attributes.

To Redefine Attributes with Attredef

- From the keyboard: **(load "<drive:>/path/attredef")**⏎
  Attredef.⏎

Table 1: Template tags and codes for extracting information about blocks

Tag	Code	Description
BL:LEVEL	N000000	Level of nesting for block
BL:NAME	C000000	Block name
BL:X	N000000	X value for block insertion point
BL:Y	N000000	Y value for block insertion point
BL:Z	N000000	Z value for block insertion point
BL:NUMBER	N000000	Block counter
BL:HANDLE	C000000	Block handle
BL:LAYER	C000000	Name of layer block is on
BL:ORIENT	N000000	Block rotation angle
BL:XSCALE	N000000	Block X scale
BL:YSCALE	N000000	Block Y scale
BL:ZSCALE	N000000	Block Z scale
BL:XEXTRUDE	N000000	X value for block extrusion direction
BL:YEXTRUDE	N000000	Y value for block extrusion direction
BL:ZEXTRUDE	N000000	Z value for block extrusion direction

Note: Italicized zeros indicate adjustable variables.

Then follow these steps:

1. **Name of block you wish to redefine:** Enter the name of an existing block. **Select new block**...

2. **Select objects:** Select the objects that are to comprise new block.

3. **Insertion base point of new block:** Enter the base point.

● **NOTES**   To use Attredef, first create the elements of the replacement block, including attribute definitions. Be sure the new attribute tags are the same as the old tags that you wish to maintain. You have to load Attredef only once per editing session. You can then use Attredef at any time.

See Also   Commands: Attdef

AUDIT

● **VERSIONS**   Version 11

● **PURPOSE**   Checks a drawing file for errors or corrupted data. If errors are detected, AutoCAD will optionally correct them.

To Use Audit

- From the keyboard: **Audit**⏎

- From the screen menu: **Utility-Audit**

Then complete the following step:

Fix errors detected? <N> Select **Yes** to correct any errors found.

If errors are detected, a screen like the one in Figure 5 will be displayed.

If no errors are detected, a screen display like the following will appear:

4 Blocks audited
Pass 1 4 entities audited
Pass 2 4 entities audited
total errors found 0 fixed 0

● **NOTES** Audit creates an ASCII file that contains a report of the audit and any action taken. The file has the extension .ADT. The information presented by the Audit command may not be important to most users. However, it may help your AutoCAD dealer or Autodesk's product support department to diagnose a problem with a file.

See Also Main menu option 9: Recover damaged drawing

```
CP,      *COPY
DV,      *DVIEW
E,       *ERASE
L,       *LINE
LA,      *LAYER
M,       *MOVE
MS,      *MSPACE
P,       *PAN
PS,      *PSPACE
PL,      *PLINE
R,       *REDRAW
Z,       *ZOOM

3DLINE, *LINE

; easy access to _PKSER (serial number) system variable
SERIAL, *_PKSER

; These are the local aliases for AutoCAD AME commands.
; Comment out any you don't want or add your own.
; Note that aliases must be typed completely.

; Primitives.

BOX,            *SOLBOX
```

Figure 5: Audit error screen (with errors)

AUTOLISP

● **VERSIONS** 2.18 and later

● **PURPOSE** AutoLISP is a programming language embedded in AutoCAD. It allows you to automate repetitive tasks and add your own custom commands to AutoCAD. AutoLISP enables you to link applications written in C to AutoCAD. Several AutoLISP programs are provided with AutoCAD, and others can be obtained from computer bulletin boards such as the Autodesk forum or CompuServe.

To Use AutoLISP

1. Enter your AutoLISP program code directly through the command prompt, or write your code with a word processor and store it as an ASCII file with the file name extension .LSP.

2. If you save your program code as a file on disk, use the AutoLISP Load function to load your program while in the AutoCAD drawing editor. The following example shows the syntax for the Load function:

   (load "<drive>/directory/filename")↵

   You can leave off the drive and directory information if either your DOS path or the Acad environment variable points to the directory that holds the AutoLISP programs.

3. Once a program file is loaded, you can use it by entering its name through the keyboard, just like a standard AutoCAD program. You don't have to load the file again while in the current editing session.

● **NOTES** You can combine your favorite AutoLISP programs into a single file called Acad.LSP. Place Acad.LSP in your AutoCAD directory. It will be loaded automatically every time you open a drawing file. AutoLISP code can also be embedded in the AutoCAD menu system. Versions 10 and 11 use AutoLISP code extensively in the standard menu. For a detailed discussion of AutoLISP, you may want to purchase this author's *ABC's of AutoLISP* (SYBEX, 1990). For information on how to edit an AutoCAD menu file, consult my *Mastering AutoCAD*, Fourth Edition (1991), or *Advanced Techniques in AutoCAD*, Second Edition (1989), by Robert M. Thomas, both published by SYBEX Inc.

AXIS

- **VERSIONS** All versions

- **PURPOSE** Displays tick marks along the bottom and right-hand edge of the drawing area. These marks help determine distances and relative locations. The marks can reflect the Snap setting or a multiple thereof.

To Activate Axis

- From the keyboard: **Axis** ↵

- From the screen menu: **Settings-Axis**

- From the pull-down menu: **Settings-Drawing tools-Drawing tools** (see Ddrmodes)

Then complete the following step:

Tick spacing(X) or ON/OFF/Snap/Aspect <default setting>: Enter the spacing of the tick marks or an option.

- **OPTIONS**

Tick spacing(X)   Sets the spacing of axis tick marks.

ON/OFF Toggles Axis command on or off.

Snap Sets axis tick mark to match Snap setting.

Aspect Allows you to set the X and Y tick mark spacing to different values.

● **NOTES** If you type a numeral followed by an **X** at the **Tick spacing** prompt, the value entered will represent a multiple of the current Snap setting. If set to **0**, the tick marks reflect the Snap settings.

If you set Axis to be a multiple of the Snap setting and change the Snap distance, Axis remains at the previous Snap setting.

See Also Commands: Ddrmodes. System variables: Axismode and Axisunit

AXROT (AUTOLISP)

● **VERSIONS** 10 and later

● **PURPOSE** Allows you to rotate an object or set of objects about the X-, Y-, or Z- axis.

To Rotate Objects Using Axrot

- From the keyboard: **(load "<drive>:/path/axrot")**↵**Axrot**↵
- From the screen menu: **Bonus-Axrot** (11)

Then folow these steps:

1. **Select objects:** Pick the objects to rotate.
2. **Degrees of rotation <0>:** Enter the rotation angle.
3. **Base point <0,0,0>:** Pick the center point of rotation.

● **NOTE**   From the keyboard, you only have to load Axrot once per editing session. You can then use Axrot at any time. It is not necessary to load Alias if you are using the menu.

See Also   AutoLISP, Rotate

BASE

● **VERSIONS**   All versions

● **PURPOSE**   When you insert one drawing into another, Base sets the drawing's *base point*, a point of reference for insertion. You select the base point in relation to the WCS (World Coordinate System). The default base point for all drawings is the WCS origin point at coordinate 0,0,0.

To Set a Base Point

- From the keyboard: **Base** ↵

- From the screen menu: **Blocks-Base**

Then complete the following step:

Base point <0.0000,0.0000,0.0000>: Enter the coordinates to pick a point.

See Also   Commands: Block, Insert, Select/Point selection

BASELINE (DIM)

● **VERSIONS**   1.4 and later

● **PURPOSE** Continues a dimension string using the first extension line of the most recently inserted dimension as its first extension line. You are prompted only for the second extension line origin. The dimension is placed above, and is parallel to, the last dimension.

Before Dimensioning

You must have issued the Dim or Dim1 command to use any dimensioning subcommand.

To Continue a Dimension from the Baseline

- From the keyboard: **Baseline** ↵

- From the screen menu: **Dim-Linear-Baseline**

Then follow these steps:

1. **Second extension line origin:** Pick a point indicating the extension line origin for a continuing dimension.

2. **Dimension text <default dimension>:** Press ↵ to accept the default dimension text, or enter new text.

● **NOTE** To continue a dimension from the baseline of an old dimension, use the Update dimension subcommand before using Baseline.

See Also Dimension Variable: Dimdli

BEGIN A NEW DRAWING

● **VERSIONS** All versions

● **PURPOSE** Lets you start a new drawing from scratch or use an existing drawing as a template for a new drawing.

To Begin a New Drawing

1. Go to the AutoCAD main menu and enter a **1** at the **Enter selection** prompt.

2. At the **Enter NAME of drawing** prompt, enter the name of your new drawing, excluding the .DWG file extension. If a drawing with the same name exists, you will get a prompt asking you if you wish to overwrite the existing file.

● **NOTES** You can use an existing drawing as a template for a new drawing. Enter the new file name, followed by an equal sign and the name of the file you wish to use as a template, as in the following example: **Enter NAME of drawing: new=template**. There should be no spaces between the equal sign and the file names. Drive and directory specifications can be included.

AutoCAD uses a file called Acad.dwg as the prototype file for all new drawings. If you want different default settings for your new drawings you can open Acad.dwg and set it up the way you want. Acad.dwg is in the AutoCAD directory or in the Support subdirectory of the AutoCAD directory.

If you have a nonstandard prototype Acad.dwg file and you want to open a file using the standard AutoCAD defaults, type an equal sign after the new file name. If you get the message that AutoCAD cannot find the prototype Acad.dwg file, you can create it by entering **ACAD=** at the **Enter NAME of drawing** prompt.

BLIPMODE OR BLIPS

● **VERSIONS** 2.1 and later

● **PURPOSE** When you draw with AutoCAD, tiny crosses called blips appear wherever you select points. These blips are not part of your drawing. They help you locate points that you have selected. You can suppress these blips if you don't want them or if you have written a macro that does not require them.

To Reset Blipmode

- From the keyboard: **Blipmode** ↵
- From the screen menu: **Settings-Blips**

Then complete the following step:

ON/OFF <current setting>: Enter the option name.

● OPTIONS

ON   Displays blips when you enter points.

OFF   Suppresses blips when you enter points.

See Also   System variables: Blipmode

BLOCK

● **VERSIONS**   All versions

● **PURPOSE**   Groups a set of drawing objects together to act as a single object. You can then insert, copy, scale, or save the block as an external file.

To Create a Block

- From the keyboard: **Block** ↵
- From the screen menu: **Blocks-Block**

Then follow these steps:

1. **Block name (or ?):** Enter the name for the block. Enter a question mark to list existing blocks.

2. **Insertion base point:** Enter a coordinate value or pick a point to set the base point of the block.

3. **Select objects:** Pick objects to include in the block.

The objects you select will disappear, but you can restore them as individual objects by issuing the Oops command.

● **NOTE** Blocks only exist within the drawing in which they are created. However, you can convert them into drawing files with the Wblock command. Blocks can also contain other blocks. You can include attributes in blocks to allow the input and storage of information; see Attdef.

If you attempt to create a block that has the same name as an existing block, you will see the prompt:

Block <name> already exists.
Redefine it? <N>

To redefine the existing block, enter **Y**. The Block command proceeds as usual and replaces the existing block with the new one. If the existing block has been inserted into the drawing, the new block appears in its place. If Regenauto has been turned off, the new block will not appear until you issue a Regen command.

See Also Commands: Attdisp, Attedit, Attext, Ddatte, Insert, Regen, Regenauto, Wildcards

BREAK

● **VERSIONS** 2.0 and later

● **PURPOSE** Erases a line, trace, circle, arc, or a two-dimensional polyline between two points.

To Use Break

● From the keyboard: **Break** ↵

- From the screen menu: **Edit-Break**

- From the pull-down menu: **Modify-Break** (11,10), **Edit-Break** (9)

Then follow these steps:

1. **Select object:** Pick an object to be broken.

2. **Second point (or F for first point):** Pick the second point of the break or enter **F** to specify the first and second points.

● **NOTES** If you use the cursor to pick the object, the "pick" point becomes the first point of the break. Pick the second point of the break or enter **F** to specify a different first break point. If you selected the object using a window, crossing window, or a Last or Previous option, you are automatically prompted for a first and second point.

Break does not work on blocks, solids, text, shapes, three-dimensional faces, or three-dimensional polylines.

You can only break objects that lie in a plane parallel to the current UCS. Also, if you are not viewing the current UCS in plan, you may get the wrong result. Use the Plan command to view the current UCS in plan.

When breaking circles, you must use the proper break point selection sequence. A counterclockwise sequence causes the break to occur between the two break points. A clockwise sequence causes the segment between the two points to remain and the rest of the circle to disappear.

Prior to version 9, ellipses break in an erratic manner. If you have problems breaking an ellipse, try making small breaks near the desired break points and then erasing the segment between them.

See Also Change, Trim, UCS

CALC (AUTOLISP)

• VERSIONS   11

• PURPOSE   Calc is an on-line calculator. It stores calculated values as variables that can be recalled any time during the current editing session.

To Use the Calculator

- From the keyboard: **(load "<drive>:/path/calc")** ⏎ **Calc** ⏎

- From the screen menu: **Bonus-Calc**

Then follow these steps:

1. **First number**: Enter a number or indicate a distance by picking two points.

2. **Calc: Clear/Exit/Mem/Sq-rt/Trig/Y^x/ or +-*/ <Clear>:**

• OPTIONS

Clear   Sets the current running total to zero.

Exit   Exits the Calc command or the current Calc mode.

Mem   Gives access to the memory options via the following prompt **Mem: Delete/Exit/List/Recall/Set or + - */ <Set>:**

Mem: Delete   Lets you set stored variable values to nil. At the prompt **Delete (All=*C):** enter the name of the variable you wish to set to nil. Enter ***C** to set all variables to nil.

Mem: List   Displays a list of variables and their values.

Mem: Recall   Sets the current running total to a saved variable value and returns you to the Calc prompt. At the prompt **Recall:** enter the name of the variable to recall.

Mem: Set   Assigns the current total to a variable. At the prompt **Set:** enter a variable name.

Sq-rt   Finds the square root of the number entered.

Trig   Allows you to enter trig functions via the prompt **Trig: ACosine ASine ATangent Cosine Sine Tangent <Exit>:** Enter the capitalized letter of the trig function you want to apply to the current total. The resulting value becomes the new total.

Y^x   Raises the current total by the power of x. Prompts you for the power of x.

+   In the Calc mode, adds the current total to another number. You are prompted for the number. In the Mem mode, + adds the current total to a variable and sets the current total and variable to the resulting value. You are prompted for a variable.

−   In the Calc mode, subtracts the next number entered from the current total. You are prompted to enter a number. In the Mem mode, − subtracts the current total from a variable and sets the total and variable to the resulting value. You are prompted for the variable.

*   In the Calc mode, multiplies a number by the current total. You are prompted for the number. In the Mem mode, * multiplies the current total by a variable and sets the total and variable to the resulting value. You are prompted for the variable.

/   In the Calc mode, divides the current total by a number. You are prompted for the number. In the Mem mode, / divides a variable by the current total and sets the total and variable to the resulting value. You are prompted for the variable.

● **NOTES**   From the keyboard, you have to load Calc only once per editing session. You can then use Calc at any time. It is not necessary to load Calc if you are using the menu.

See Also   AutoLISP

CATALOG

● **VERSIONS**   2.1 and later

● **PURPOSE**   Catalog displays a list of files in any specified drive or directory. You get the same list in DOS when you enter **dir** /w. At the **Files** prompt, enter any drive letter, directory name, or wildcard character, as you would in DOS. If you give no specifications, Catalog displays the list for the current drive.

To View a Catalog

● From the keyboard: **Catalog** ↵

● From the screen menu: **Utility-External Command-Catalog**

Then complete the following step:

Files: Enter standard DOS file names; wildcard characters are accepted.

See Also   Dir, Files

CENTER (DIM)

● **VERSIONS**   2.0 and later

● **PURPOSE**   Center places a cross at the center point of a selected arc or circle. To choose center lines instead of a center cross, use the Dimcen dimension variable (see Dim Vars).

Before Dimensioning

You must have issued the Dim or Dim1 command to use any dimensioning subcommand.

To Mark the Center of an Arc or Circle

* From the keyboard: **Center** ↵

* From the screen menu: **Dim-Center** (9,10), **Dim-Radial-Center** (11)

Then complete the following step:

   Select arc or circle: <arc or circle>

See Also   Dimension Variables: Dimcen

CFIG386.EXE

* **VERSIONS**   10 and 11, 386 version

* **PURPOSE**   The Cfig386.EXE utility is a stand-alone application that controls AutoCAD386's memory use.

To Use Cfig386.EXE

At the DOS prompt, enter the following: **Cfig386 ACAD <optional switches>**. If you do not enter the optional switches, a listing of the current switch settings appears. The default listing looks like this:

```
-minswfsize 400000
-swapdefdisk
-swapchk off
-intmap 8
vscan 20000
```

• OPTIONS

-b0 Lets AutoCAD 386 run on the Intel B0 80386 microprocessor.

- clear Clears all the switch settings. If you use this option, you must reset the minimum switch settings by entering **cfig386 acad -minswfsize 400000 -swapdefdisk -dwapchk off -intmap 8 - vscan 20000**

-extlow/-exthigh Controls the amount and location of extended memory the DOS extender uses. These switches take hex numbers as arguments. The -extlow switch sets the low address and -exthigh sets the high address.

-intmap/-primap Prevents the DOS extender from using reloca- tion interrupt vectors. -primap disables the remapping of the BIOS print screen function call.

-maxvcpi Limits the amount of memory taken from EMS emulators that use the VCPI interface. This switch takes as an argu- ment a number representing the number of bytes to allocate to AutoCAD.

-minreal /-maxreal Sets the amount of standard DOS memory left free by the DOS extender. -minreal sets the minimum amount of memory to leave free and -maxreal sets the maximum.

-minswfsize Sets the minimum required swap file size. If AutoCAD doesn't find the amount of space specified by this switch, an error message appears and AutoCAD is aborted.

-maxswfize Sets the maximum swap file size. If not set, AutoCAD uses all available free disk space.

-nopgexp Causes AutoCAD to load all of the AutoCAD ex- ecutable files from disk. This can help speed AutoCAD on networks where the program resides on a server.

-swapchk Determines when and how the size of the AutoCAD swap file is to be increased. When set to on, -swapchk returns an out-of-swap-space error message. Set to off, no message is returned.

When -swapchk is set to max, AutoCAD makes the swap file as large as the virtual address space used (see Status). If -swapchk is not set, the default swap file setting has force, causing the swap file to be increased in size as needed. The size is increased only by the amount of virtual memory allocated minus the amount of physical memory available.

-swapdisk   Sets the root directory of the current default drive as the location for swap files.

-swapdir   Lets you specify a drive and directory for swap files.

-vdisk   Corrects problems with some ramdisk software Auto-CAD 386 has difficulty with.

-vscan   Sets how frequently AutoCAD checks memory allocation for paging purposes. The setting accepts a number representing milliseconds. The minimum value allowed is 1000 ms, which equals 1 second.

To alter a switch setting, enter the switch name, followed by a space and the new switch setting, as in **Cfig386 Acad <switch_name> <new_switch_setting>**

● **NOTES**   Not all the switch options are listed here. Some are intended for programmers and require lengthy explanation. For more on Cfig386, consult your AutoCAD installation and performance guide.

See Also   Command: Status

CHAMFER

● **VERSIONS**   2.5 and later

● **PURPOSE**   Chamfer joins two nonparallel lines with an intermediate line, or adds intermediate lines between the line segments of a two-dimensional polyline. The Distance option sets the length of the intermediate line.

To Use Chamfer

- From the keyboard: **Chamfer** ↵

- From the screen menu: **Edit-Chamfer**

- From the pull-down menu: **Modify-Chamfer**

Then follow these steps:

1. **Polyline/Distance/<select first line>:** Pick the first line.

2. **Select second line:** Pick the second line.

● OPTIONS

Polyline   Allows you to chamfer all line segments within a polyline. This option prompts you to select a two-dimensional polyline. All the joining polyline segments are then chamfered.

Distance   Allows you to specify the length of the chamfer. This option prompts you for the first and second chamfer distance. These are the distances from the intersection point of the lines to the beginning of the chamfer.

● NOTES   You can chamfer only objects that lie in a plane parallel to the current user coordinate system (UCS). Also, if you are not viewing the current UCS in plan, you may get the wrong result. Use the Plan command to view the current UCS in plan, then use the Chamfer command.

Version 11 users can preset chamfer distances by picking the Chamfer Distance option on the Options pull-down menu.

See Also   Fillet. System Variables: Chamfera, Chamferb

CHANGE

• **VERSIONS**   All versions; Thickness and Elevation options added in version 2.1. Layer option at the **Properties** prompt dropped in version 11.

• **PURPOSE**   Change can alter several properties of an object. You can change all the properties of lines. Move line end points by selecting a point at the first prompt in the Change command. If you select several lines, all of the end points closest to the selected point move to the new point. If the Ortho mode is on, the lines become parallel and their end points align with the selected point.

You can change the color, layer, or line type of arcs, circles, and polylines. You can also change the rotation angle or layer assignment of a block.

To Change the Properties of an Object

• From the keyboard: **Change** ⏎

• From the screen menu: **Edit-Change**

Then follow these steps:

1.   **Select objects:** Select objects to be changed.

2.   **Properties/<change point>:** If the object is a line, its rotation angle can be changed. Otherwise, enter **P** to change the property of the selected object(s).

3.   If you select the Properties option (**Change what property (Color/Elev/LAyer/LType/Thickness) ?**), enter the desired option.

• **OPTIONS**

Properties   Changes the color, elevation, layer, line type, or thickness of an object.

Color   Prompts you for color to change selected objects to.

LAyer   Prompts you for a new layer.

LType   Prompts you for a new line type.

Thickness   Prompts you for a new thickness in the object's Z-axis.

● **NOTES**   The Thickness option will extrude a two-dimensional line, arc, circle, or polyline into the Z-axis. Thickness does not work on blocks, however.

In versions prior to 11, the Elevation option changes an object's location in the Z-axis. The Elevation option does not work on objects that are not in a plane parallel to the current UCS.

Change can alter text style, height, rotation angle, or the text itself.

When you change an object's color, the object no longer has the color of the layer on which it resides. This can be confusing in complex drawings. To make an object the same color as its layer, enter **Bylayer** at the **Color** prompt.

See Also   Color, Elev, Chprop, UCS, Select

CHBLOCK (AUTOLISP)

● **VERSIONS**   11

● **PURPOSE**   Changes the X, Y, or Z scale of a block, a block's insertion point, or a rotation angle.

To Use Chblock

● From the keyboard: **(load "<drive>:/path/chblock")** ↵, **Chb** ↵

Then follow these steps:

1. **Select objects:** Pick the block to edit.

2. **Insertion point/Rotation/Scale/<Exit>:** Enter the option.

● OPTIONS

Insertion point   Lets you relocate a block.

Rotation   Lets you change the rotation angle of a block. You are prompted for a new rotation angle.

Scale   Lets you change the X, Y, or Z scale of a block via the prompt:

BLOCK SCALES: X-1.00 Y-1.00 Z-1.00
Change scale. All/X/Y/Z/<Exit>:

Scale: All   Lets you change the X, Y, and Z scales of the block to the same value.

Scale: X/Y/Z   Lets you change the X, Y, or Z scales of the block individually.

● **NOTES**   From the keyboard, you have to load Chblock only once per editing session. You then can use Chblock at any time. It is not necessary to load Chblock if you are using the menu.

See Also   AutoLISP, Block, Insert, Wblock

CHFACE

● **VERSIONS**   10 and later

● **PURPOSE**   Moves a vertex of a 3dface that is overlapping another 3dface.

To Move a 3dface Vertex

- From the keyboard: **Chface** ⏎

- From the screen menu: **Bonus-Chface** (11 only)

Then follow these steps:

1. **Select entity to change:** Pick a 3dface to edit.

2. **1/2/3/4/Undo/Display/<Select vertex>:** Enter the desired option or pick the vertex to move. If you pick a vertex, you are prompted for a new location.

● OPTIONS

1/2/3/4   Selects a vertex based on its number. After you enter a number, you are prompted for a new location of the vertex.

Undo   Rescinds in reverse order the Chface options you have entered.

Display   Refreshes the display, like a redraw.

See Also   3dface, Mesh. System Variables: Splframe

CHPROP

- **VERSIONS**   10 and later

- **PURPOSE**   Chprop works like the Change/Properties command, except that Chprop allows you to change the properties of all object types regardless of their three-dimensional orientation. However, the Elevation option is not offered. Use the Move command in place of the Elevation option.

To Change an Object's Properties

- From the keyboard: **Chprop** ⏎

- From the screen menu: **Edit-Chprop**

- From the pull-down menu: **Modify-Properties** (10)

Then follow these steps:

1. **Select objects:** Select objects whose properties you wish to modify.

2. **Change what property (Color/LAyer/LType/Thickness) ?** Enter the option.

● OPTIONS

Color   Prompts you for a color to which selected objects will be changed.

LAyer   Prompts you for a new layer.

LType   Prompts you for a new line type.

Thickness   Prompts you for new thickness in the object's Z-axis.

See Also   Change, Color, Elev, Select, UCS

CHTEXT

● VERSIONS   11

● **PURPOSE**   Changes text wording, justification, height, width, location, rotation angle, and style.

To Change Text

- From the keyboard: **(load "<drive>:/path/chtext")** ⏎ **Cht** ⏎

- From the screen menu: **Bonus-Chtext**

Then follow these steps:

1. **Select objects:** Select the text you wish to edit. You can select more than one text entity.

2. **Height/Justification/Location/Rotation/Style/Text/ Undo/Width:** Enter the desired option.

● OPTIONS

Height   Changes the height of the selected text. If you select more than one text entity, the following prompt appears:

Individual/List/<New height for all text entities>:

Enter desired height for all text or enter a desired option. If you select only one text entity, you are prompted for a new text height.

Height:Individual   Changes the height of an individual text entity. The text is highlighted and you are prompted for a new height.

Height:List   Displays the minimum, maximum, and average height of the selected group of text entities.

Justification   Changes the justification of the selected text, via the prompt:

Justification point(s) - Aligned/Center/Fit/Left/Middle/ Right/<?>:

Enter the desired justification style. See Text and Dtext for available justification styles.

Location   Moves text to a new location, based on the text insertion point.

Rotation   Changes the rotation angle of text. As with the Height option, you can change the rotation angle of all the selected text at once, or of individual text entities. You can also get a list of the minimum, maximum, and average rotation angle.

Style   Changes the style of the selected text, either all the selected text at once, or each text entity individually. It can also list styles used by the selected text entities.

Text   Changes the wording of text, via the prompt:

Search and replace text. Individually/Retype/<Globally>:

Use the Individually option to change the wording of text entities one at a time. You can use either the text editing dialog box or specify a string to be replaced. Retype replaces an entire line with a new line. Globally replaces all occurrences of a string (the Match string) in the selected set of text entities. You are prompted for a Match string and a New string of replacement text.

Undo   Rescinds the edits you have made since you started the Chtext command.

Width   Changes the width factor of the selected text, either all at once, or individually for each text entity. Width can also provide a list of the minimum, maximum, and average width used by the selected set of text entities.

● Notes   From the keyboard, you have to load Chtext only once per editing session. You then can use Chtext at any time. It is not necessary to load Chtext if you are using the menu.

CL (AUTOLISP)

● VERSIONS   10 and later

● PURPOSE   Draws a pair of center lines through an arc or circle.

To Create Centerlines
- From the keyboard: **(load "drive:/path/cl")**⏎ **Cl** ⏎

- From the screen menu: **Bonus-Cl** (11)

Then follow these steps:

1. **Select arc or circle:** Pick the arc or circle.

2. **Radius is ### Length/<Extension>:** Enter the distance you want the center line to extend beyond the circumference of the arc or circle, or enter **L** to specify the overall length of a center line from the center.

● **NOTES**   From the keyboard, you have to load C1 only once per editing session. You then can use C1 at any time. It is not necessary to load C1 if you are using a menu.

See Also   Dim-Center

COLOR

● **VERSIONS**   2.5 and later

● **PURPOSE**   Sets the color of objects being drawn. Once you select a color with the Color command, all objects will be given the selected color regardless of their layers, unless you specify Bylayer as the color. Objects you drew before using the Color command are not affected.

To Set the Color of Objects

- From the keyboard: **Color** ↵

- From the screen menu: **Settings-Color**

- From the pull-down menu: **Modes-Entity Creation** (9), **Settings-Entity Creation** (10), **Options-Entity Creation** (11)

Then complete the following step:

> **New entity color <current default>:** Enter the color.

When using the pull-down menu, you will get a dialog box with a color input box. You can enter the name or number of a color in this dialog box.

● OPTIONS

Table 2 contains the color names that AutoCAD recognizes, and their number codes. In addition to these names, you can enter any number from 1 to 255. The color that is displayed depends on your display adapter and monitor, but the first seven colors are the same for most display systems.

● **NOTES** Bylayer gives objects the color of the layer on which they are placed. It is the default color setting. Byblock works on objects used in blocks. If such an object is assigned the Byblock color, it will take on the color of the layer in which the block is placed.

Table 2: Color names recognized by AutoCAD

Color Name	Color Number
red	1
yellow	2
green	3
cyan	4
blue	5
magenta	6
white	7

Command	Color
Bylayer	color of the layer the object is on
Byblock	color of the layer a block is on

Assign colors carefully, especially if you use them to distinguish different layers.

See Also Change/Properties/Color, Chprop/Color, Layer

COMPILE SHAPE/FONT DESCRIPTION FILE

- **VERSION** All versions

- **PURPOSE** You can create your own text fonts and shapes by compiling a shape/font description file. This file is an ASCII file that uses a special system of codes to describe your fonts or shapes. Option 7 on the main menu converts this ASCII file into a form that lets AutoCAD read the descriptions and include them in a drawing.

To Compile Your Own Text Fonts

1. Enter option **7** at the main menu.

2. Enter the name of the font or shape file to be converted.

CONFIGURE AUTOCAD

- **VERSIONS** All versions

- **PURPOSE** You can configure AutoCAD for specific input and output devices and display systems. You can also control plotting optimization and aspect ratio, screen aspect ratio, network capabilites, the location of temporary files, and much more.

To Configure AutoCAD

1. Go to AutoCAD's main menu. At the **Enter selection** prompt, enter **5**. A screen appears showing the current configuration.

2. Press ⏎ to go to the Configuration menu. Enter the number of the configuration option you wish to access.

3. After you have gone through the configuration, you are returned to the Configuration menu. You can enter the number of another configuration option or enter **0** to exit the configuration menu and return to the main menu.

4. After you enter 0, you are prompted to save the configuration changes you have just made. Press ⏎ to accept the changes or enter **N** to cancel the changes and return to the previous settings.

● OPTIONS

0. Exit to main menu   Lets you exit the configuration menu. You are then asked whether you want to save your configuration changes.

1. Show current configuration   Displays the current configuration.

2. Allow detailed configuration   Gives you access to more detailed configuration options. These include plotter optimization and the control of the display colors on color systems.

3. Configure video display   Lets you control the aspect ratio of your drawing editor screen. You can also turn on or off the various parts of the drawing editor screen. You can control the colors shown in the drawing editor if you select option 2 before picking this option.

4. Configure digitizer   Lets you control the sensitivity of your pointing device. If you use a digitizer, you can change the puck configuration. Port assignments can also be controlled through this option.

5. Configure Plotter   Lets you adjust the plotter output aspect ratio and change port assignments. If you use option 2 before issuing this option, you can also control pen optimization. Most of the other options can also be changed using the Plot command. To adjust the aspect ratio, draw a square that measures 5 units by 5 units. Use this square to help adjust the plotter aspect ratio.

6. Configure printer plotter Lets you adjust the printer output aspect ratio and change port assignments. Other options can also be changed using the Prplot command. To adjust the aspect ratio, draw a square that measures 5 units by 5 units. Use this square to help adjust the printer aspect ratio.

7. Configure system console Not applicable to IBM-type computers.

8. Configure operating parameters Lets you control a variety of default settings and network features, as follows:

- Alarm on error turns on a beep sound when errors occur.

- Initial drawing setup lets you use a prototype drawing file other than the standard Acad.DWG.

- Default plot file name lets you specify a plot-to-file file name extension.

- Plot spooler directory lets you specify a directory in which to store your plot files. Some plot spooling software periodically checks a directory and automatically plots new files that appear there.

- Placing Temporary Files lets you specify where AutoCAD is to place temporary files. For non-386 versions, directing AutoCAD to store temporary files in a RAM disk can improve overall speed. This option is also useful in networks.

- Network node name lets you segregate temporary files by specifying a unique filename extension. This is useful when several people are working on files in the same directory of a network server.

- AutoLISP feature lets you enable or disable AutoLISP.

- Full-time CRC (Cyclic Redundancy Check) validation lets you control an error checking mechanism built into AutoCAD.

- Automatic auditing controls the auditing of imported files of the DXF, DXB, or Iges file type (see Audit).

- Login name is used to specify the login name of AutoCAD nodes on a network.

- Server authorization and file locking lets you control the file locking function of AutoCAD and allows updating of server authorization codes when network nodes are added.

CHANGING HARDWARE

When you first install AutoCAD, you are asked to specify a video display, pointing device, plotter, and printer plotter. If you change your display or input/output hardware, you must run the appropriate configuration option to inform AutoCAD of the change.

KEEPING MULTIPLE CONFIGURATIONS

You can use DOS to maintain several AutoCAD configurations. AutoCAD stores configuration information in a set of files. You can use the Acadcfg DOS environment variable to store these files in a specific directory.

First, for each set of configuration files, add subdirectories under the Acad directory. For example, you might create a subdirectory called Standard and another called Present. Then, tell AutoCAD where to look for the configuration files, using the DOS Set command and the Acadcfg environment variable. For example, to store a configuration for the standard screen setup, enter the following command line at the DOS prompt:

SET ACADCFG=C:\ACAD\STANDARD

When AutoCAD starts, it will look in the Acad\Standard directory for the configuration files.

You will receive a message that AutoCAD is not yet configured. As yet there are no configuration files in the directories. Now, configure AutoCAD as already described.

Again, use the DOS Set command, but this time direct AutoCAD to look in a different directory for the configuration files:

SET ACADCFG=C:\ACAD\PRESENT

Set up another configuration for AutoCAD. When all this is done, you will be able to switch between the two configurations just by resetting Acadcfg before you start AutoCAD. Adding these Acadcfg settings to a batch file will further simplify configuration switching.

CONTINUE (DIM)

● **VERSIONS**   1.4 and later

● **PURPOSE**   Continues a dimension string by using the second extension line of the most recently inserted dimension as its first extension line. You are only prompted for the second extension line origin. The dimension is placed inline with and is parallel to the last dimension. You can also enter Continue as **Con** at the **Dim** prompt.

Before Dimensioning

You must have issued the Dim or Dim1 command to use any dimensioning subcommand.

To Continue a Dimension

● From the keyboard: **Continue** ⏎

● From the screen menu: **Dim-Linear-Continue**

Then follow these steps:

1. **Second extension line origin:** Pick a point indicating the extension line origin for a continuing dimension. The second extension line of the last dimension entered will be used as the first extension line.

2.   **Dimension text <default dimension>:** Press ↵ to accept the default dimension text or enter new dimension text.

● **NOTE**   To continue a dimension from the last extension line of an old dimension, use the Update dimension subcommand before using Continue.

See Also   Dimension Variable: Dimdli

CONVERT OLD DRAWING FILE

● **VERSIONS**   All versions

● **PURPOSE**   Updates older AutoCAD drawing files.

To Convert an Old Drawing File

1.   Enter option 8 at the main menu.

2.   Enter the name of the file you wish to update.

● **NOTES**   In most cases, you don't have to update files from older versions of AutoCAD. Usually, it is only necessary when you are updating across several versions of AutoCAD. Once you update a file, you cannot edit that file using an earlier version of AutoCAD.

See Also   Recover

COPY

- **VERSIONS**   All versions

- **PURPOSE**   Copies a single object or a set of objects.

To Copy

- From the keyboard: **Copy** ↵

- From the screen menu: **Edit-Copy**

- From the pull-down menu: **Edit-Copy** (9), **Modify-Copy** (10, 11)

Then follow these steps:

1. **Select objects:** Select objects to be copied.

2. **<Base point or displacement>/Multiple** Pick the reference or "base" point for the copy or enter **M** for multiple copies.

3. **Second point of displacement:** Pick the copy distance and direction in relation to base point or enter the displacement value.

- **OPTIONS**

Multiple   Allows you to make several copies of the selected objects. The second point is repeated until you press ↵ or **Ctrl-C.**

- **NOTES**   AutoCAD assumes you want to make copies within the current UCS. However, you can make copies in three-dimensional space by entering X,Y,Z coordinates or by using the Osnap overrides to pick objects in three-dimensional space.

If you press ↵ at the **Second point** prompt without entering a point value, the selected objects may be copied to an area that is off your current drawing. To recover use the U or Undo command.

- **SEE ALSO**   Array, Auto, Multiple, Select

DBLIST

- **VERSIONS**   All versions

- **PURPOSE**   Lists the properties of all objects in a drawing.

To List Properties of Objects

- From the keyboard: **Dblist** ⏎

- From the screen menu: **Inquiry-Dblist**

- **NOTES**   When you invoke Dblist the screen switches to Text mode and the list of objects scrolls down the screen. Press **Ctrl-C** to stop the listing. Dblist is similar to the List command.

See Also   ID, List

DDATTE

- **VERSIONS**   9 and later

- **PURPOSE**   Changes the attribute values of a single block. Ddatte displays all of the attributes in a block in a dialog box for viewing and editing.

To Edit Attribute Values

- From the keyboard: **Ddatte** ⏎

- From the screen menu: **Edit-Ddatte**

Then follow these steps:

1. **Select block:** Pick the block containing the attribute(s) to edit.

2. A dialog box appears containing the attribute prompts and values. To change an attribute value, highlight the attribute and type a new value. When you start typing, two buttons appear to the right of the attribute. Pick the OK button to confirm your edit or the Cancel button to retain the original attribute value.

● **NOTES**   If you need to edit or browse through several attributes, you can use Ddatte together with the Multiple command. At the **Command** prompt type **Multiple**, then **Ddatte**. Every time you finish editing or browsing through one block, AutoCAD will prompt you to select a block rather than return you to the **Command** prompt. To exit the Ddatte command, enter **Ctrl-C**.

Version 11 allows you to edit the existing attribute text by positioning the cursor at the appropriate location, deleting text, and typing your correction. In versions 9 and 10, you must retype the entire text string.

See Also   Attdef, Attedit, Multiple

DDEDIT

● **VERSIONS**   11

● **PURPOSE**   Changes a text or attribute definition. Ddedit displays a line of text in a dialog box for editing and viewing. You can position a cursor to delete single characters, make corrections, or add to the text.

To Edit Text Objects

- From the keyboard: **Ddedit** ↵

- From the screen menu: **Edit-Ddedit**

Then follow these steps:

1. **<Select a TEXT or ATTDEF object>/Undo:** Pick the line of text to edit.

2. A dialog box appears containing the selected text.

● **NOTES**   Every time you finish editing one line of text, AutoCAD will then prompt you to select another text or Attdef object rather than return you to the **Command** prompt. To exit the Ddedit command, press ↵ at the **select a text** prompt.

See Also   Change, Chtext (AutoLISP)

DDEMODES

● **VERSIONS**   9 and later

● **PURPOSE**   Opens a dialog box that sets several entity creation modes including default color, line type, elevation, and thickness of objects being drawn, as well as the current default layer. When preceded with an apostrophe (from the keyboard) or issued from the menu system, Ddemodes can be used transparently to change the Entity Creation mode while in another command. You can also use the Color, Linetype, Elev, Layer, and Style (11) commands to set these modes individually.

To Open the Ddemodes Dialog Box

- From the keyboard: **Ddemodes** ↵ or **'Ddemodes** ↵

- From the screen menu: **Settings-Ddemode**

- From the pull-down menu: **Modes-Entity-Creation** (9),
  Settings-Entity Creation (10), **Option-Entity Creation** (11)

● OPTIONS

When you issue Ddemodes, a dialog box appears containing the following options. For each option, an input box allows you to either select an item or enter a distance or coordinate value.

Color   Sets the current default color for objects being drawn.

Layer name   Sets the current layer.

Linetype   Sets the current default line type for objects being drawn.

Elevation   Sets the current default elevation of objects being drawn. This elevation value is the distance in the Z-axis from the X-Y plane of the current user coordinate system (UCS).

Text Style   Sets the current default text style (version 11).

Thickness   Sets the default thickness of objects being drawn. This value is a distance along the Z-axis of the object.

OK   Implements the settings displayed in the dialog box and exits the dialog box.

Cancel   Exits the dialog box without implementing any changes.

● NOTES   The default value for the color and line type setting is Bylayer, which sets an object color or line type to that of the layer in which it is placed.

See Also   Change, Color, Elev, Layer, Linetype

DDLMODES

- **VERSIONS**   9 and later

- **PURPOSE**   Displays a dialog box for control of layers. When preceded with an apostrophe (from the keyboard) or selected from the menu system, Ddlmodes allows you to change the layer settings while in another command.

To Invoke Ddlmodes Layer Control

- From the keyboard: **Ddlmodes** ↵ or **'Ddlmodes** ↵

- From the screen menu: **Layers-Ddlmodes**

- From the pull-down menu: **Modes-Modify Layer** (9), **Settings-Modify Layer** (10), **Settings-Layer Control** (11)

- **OPTIONS**

Ddlmodes opens a dialog box containing the following options. For each option an input box allows you to either pick an item or enter a value.

Current   Selects the current layer. An X or check mark appears by the current layer name.

Layer name   Changes the existing layer name.

Color   Changes the color of a layer. When an item in this column is picked, another dialog box appears that allows you to select from a list of colors.

Linetype   Changes the line type of a layer. When you pick an item in this column another dialog box appears that allows you to select from a list of line types.

New layer   Lets you add new layers.

OK   Implements the settings in the dialog box and closes the dialog box.

Cancel   Exits the dialog box without implementing any changes.

The following options appear only in versions 9 and 10. They are replaced by a scroll bar in version 11.

> **ON**   Turns layer on or off.
>
> **Frozen**   Freezes or thaws a layer.
>
> **Up**   Scrolls the list of layers up one position.
>
> **Page up**   Scrolls list of layers up one page.
>
> **Down**   Scrolls list of layers down one position.
>
> **Page down**   Scrolls list of layers down one page.

The following options appear only in version 11. The VP Frz options only affect drawings that use Paperspace in conjunction with multiple viewports.

> **Global/On**   Turns a layer on or off for all viewports.
>
> **Global/Frz**   Freezes or thaws a layer for all viewports.
>
> **VP Frz/Cur**   Freezes or thaws a layer for the current Modelspace viewport only. This setting overrides global settings.
>
> **VP Frz/New**   Causes a layer to be automatically frozen in any newly created viewport.

● **NOTES**   If you select the Color or Linetype pick box, another dialog box appears containing a selection list of available colors or line types.

Ddlmode differs from the Layer command in that line types are not automatically loaded when you select a line type for a layer. To use the Modify Layer dialog box to select line types, first use the Linetype command to load the desired line types.

See Also   Layer, Linetype, Mspace, Mview, Pspace, Rename, Viewports, Vplayer. System Variables: Tilemode

DDRMODES

- **VERSIONS** 9 and later

- **PURPOSE** Changes several mode settings at once through a dialog box. If you precede the command name with an apostrophe (from the keyboard) or select from the menu system, Ddrmodes allows you to change the mode settings while in another command.

To Open the Ddrmodes Dialog Box

- From the keyboard: **Ddrmodes** ⏎ or **'Ddrmodes** ⏎

- From the screen menu: **Settings-Ddrmode**

- From the pull-down menu: **Modes-Drawing Aids** (9), **Settings-Drawing Aids** (10), **Settings-Drawing Tools** (11)

- **OPTIONS**

When you issue Ddrmodes, the following options appear as input boxes in which you can either select an option or enter a distance value.

X Spacing Sets spacing in the X-axis for the mode under which the input box is found.

Y Spacing Sets spacing in the Y-axis for the mode under which the input box is found.

Snap angle Sets snap angle.

Snap X Base Sets Snap base point's X coordinate.

Snap Y Base Sets Snap base point's Y coordinate.

Snap Toggles Snap mode on or off. The F9 function key or the Ctrl-B combination performs the same function.

Grid   Toggles Grid mode on or off. The F7 function key or the Ctrl-G combination performs the same function.

Axis   Toggles Axis mode on or off.

Ortho   Toggles Ortho mode on or off. The F9 function key or the Ctrl-O combination performs the same function.

Blips   Toggles Blip mode on or off.

Isoplane Left   Moves an isometric cursor to the left plane.

Isoplane Top   Moves an isometric cursor to the top plane.

Isoplane Right   Moves an isometric cursor to the right plane.

Isometric   Toggles the Isometric Snap mode on or off.

OK   Implements the settings displayed in the dialog box and exits the dialog box.

Cancel   Exits the dialog box without implementing any changes.

See Also   Axis, Blipmode, Grid, Isoplane, Ortho, Snap, Snap/Style

DDUCS

● **VERSIONS**   10 and later

● **PURPOSE**   Accesses AutoCAD's user coordinate functions through a dialog box. In version 11, it sets the UCS for the current Paper/Modelspace.

To Open the Dducs Dialog Box

- From the keyboard: **Dducs** ↵
- From the screen menu: **UCS-Dducs**

- From the pull-down menu: **Settings-UCS Dialog** (10), **Settings-UCS Control** (11)

● OPTIONS

Current   Selects the UCS to be made current.

UCS Name   Displays names of defined UCS's. Changes UCS names.

List   Displays information about the UCS.

Delete   Deletes the UCS.

Define new current UCS   Displays a dialog box for defining a new UCS. All UCS command options are in this dialog box.

OK   Changes the current UCS settings to those shown in the dialog box and closes the dialog box.

Cancel   Ignores any changes entered into the dialog box and closes the dialog box.

The following options only appear in version 10. They are replaced by a scroll bar in version 11.

Up   Scrolls the UCS list up one position.

Page Up   Scrolls the UCS list up one page.

Down   Scrolls the UCS list down one position.

Page down   Scrolls the UCS list down one page.

See Also   Dview, Elev, Plan, Rename., Thickness, UCS, Vpoint. System Variables: Ucsfollow, Ucsicon, Ucsname, Ucsorg, Ucsxdir, Ucsydir, Worlducs

DEL

● VERSIONS   2.1 and later

- **PURPOSE**   Deletes files from a specified disk. At the **Files to delete** prompt, enter any drive letter or directory name.

To Delete a File

- From the keyboard: **Del** ↵

- From the screen menu: **Utility-External Command-Del**

Then complete the following step:

File to delete: Enter the file name.

See Also   Commands: Files

DELLAYER AUTOLISP

- **VERSIONS**   10 and later

- **PURPOSE**   Erases all entities on a specified layer.

To Erase Using Dellayer

- From the keyboard: (**load "<drive>:/<path>/dellayer"**)↵ **dellayer** ↵

- From the screen menu: **Bonus-Dellayer** (11)

Then complete the following step:

Layer to delete?: Enter the name of the layer whose entities you wish to delete.

- **Notes**   From the keyboard, you have to load Dellayer only once per editing session. You can then use Dellayer at any time. It is not necessary to load Dellayer if you are using the menu.

See Also   AutoLISP, SSX (AutoLISP)

DIAMETER (DIM)

- **VERSIONS**   1.4 and later

- **PURPOSE**   Adds a diameter dimension to arcs and circles.

Before Dimensioning

You must have issued the Dim or Dim1 command to use any dimensioning subcommand.

To Dimension an Arc or Circle Diameter

- From the keyboard: **Diameter** ↵

- From the screen menu: **Dim-diameter** (9,10), **Dim-Radial-Diameter** (11)

Then follow these steps:

1. **Select arc or circle:** Enter **arc** or **circle**, as appropriate.

2. **Dimension text <default dimension>:** Press ↵ to accept the default dimension text or enter dimension text.

3. **Enter leader length for text:** Pick a point that indicates the location of the leader from the dimension to the arc or circle. In versions 10 and earlier, this prompt does not appear. Instead, if the arc or circle is too small, you will get the following prompt:

    Text does not fit.
    Enter leader length for text:

Pick a point representing the length of text leader or enter a value. A leader line is drawn from the pick point at the length specified. The direction of the leader is toward the center point. A center mark is also placed at the center of the arc or circle.

● **NOTES**   The point at which you pick the arc or circle deter-mines one end of the dimension arrow. If you want the dimension to be in a horizontal or vertical orientation, use the Quadpoint Osnap override. Pick the left or right quadpoint for a horizontal dimension; pick the top or bottom quadpoint for a vertical dimension. If the Dimtix dimension variable is set to on, step 3 is omitted.

See Also   Dimcen, Dimtix

DIM/DIM1

● **VERSIONS**   All versions for Dim, version 2.5 and later for Dim1

● **PURPOSE**   Dim and Dim1 let you add dimensions to a draw-ing. Once you issue either of these commands, you can issue any dimensioning subcommand.

To Issue a Dimensioning Subcommand

● From the keyboard: **Dim** ↵ or **Dim1** ↵

● From the screen menu: **Dim-Dim** or **Dim-Dim1**

● From the pull-down menu: **Draw-Dim** (11)

Then complete the following step:

Dim: Enter any dimensioning subcommand.

● OPTIONS

See *Notes*.

● **NOTES**   AutoCAD generally uses the same types of dimensions and dimension label components as standard drafting. Figure 6 gives examples of the five types of dimensions possible in AutoCAD drawings: linear, angular, diametric, radial, and ordinate.

Dimension labels consist of the elements illustrated in Figure 7.

Table 3 describes variables that control the way AutoCAD draws dimensions. These variables control extension line and text

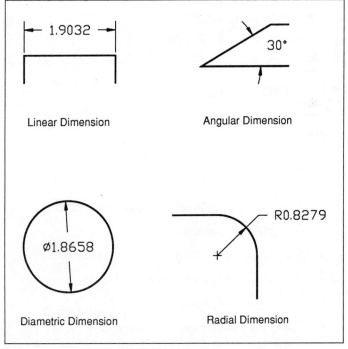

| Linear Dimension | Angular Dimension |
| Diametric Dimension | Radial Dimension |

Figure 6:   Types of dimensions

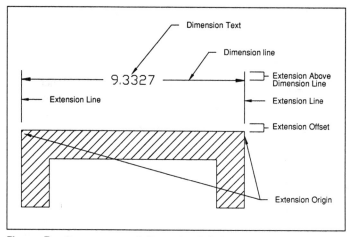

Figure 7: Components of dimension labels

Table 3: The dimension variables

Variable	Version Introduced	Description
Dimalt	2.5	When on, dimension texts for two measurement systems are inserted simultaneously (*alt*ernate). Dimaltf and Dimaltd must also be set appropriately. The alternate dimension is placed within brackets. Angular dimensions are not affected. This variable is commonly used when inches and metric units must be displayed at the same time in a dimension. The default setting is off.
Dimaltd	2.5	When Dimalt is on, Dimaltd controls the number of decimal places the alternate dimension will have (*alt*ernate *d*ecimal places). The default value is 2.

Table 3: The dimension variables (cont'd)

Variable	Version Introduced	Description
Dimaltf	2.5	When Dimalt is on, Dimaltf controls the multiplication factor for the alternate dimension (*alternate factor*). The value held by Dimaltf will be multiplied by the standard dimension value to determine the alternate dimension. The default value is 25.4, the number required to display metric units.
Dimapost	2.6	When Dimalt is on, you can use Dimapost to append text to the alternate dimension (*alternate post*). For example, if Dimapost is given the value "mm," the alternate dimension will appear as *value*mm instead of just *value.* The default value is null. To change a previously set value to null, enter a period for the Dimapost new value.
Dimaso	2.6	When on, dimensions will be associative (*associative*). When off, dimensions will consist of separate drawing entities with none of the associative dimension properties. The default is on.
Dimasz	1.4	Sets the size of dimension arrows or Dimblks (*arrow size*. See Dimblk). If set to 0, a tick is drawn in place of an arrow. The default value is .18 units.

Table 3: The dimension variables (cont'd)

Variable	Version Introduced	Description
Dimblk	2.5	You can replace the standard AutoCAD dimension arrow with one of your own design by creating a drawing of your symbol and making it a block. You then give Dimblk the name of your symbol block. This block must be drawn corresponding to a one by one unit area and must be oriented as the right side arrow. The default value is null.
Dimblk1	10	With Dimsah set to on, you can replace the standard AutoCAD dimension arrows with two different arrows using Dimblk1 and Dimblk2. Dimblk1 holds the name of the block defining the first dimension arrow while Dimblk2 holds the name of the second dimension arrow block.
Dimblk2	10	See Dimblk1.
Dimcen	1.4	Sets the size of center marks used during the Center, Diameter, and Radius dimension subcommands. A negative value draws center lines instead of the center mark cross, while a 0 value draws nothing. The default value is 0.09 units.

Table 3: The dimension variables (cont'd)

Variable	Version Introduced	Description
Dimdle	2.5	With Dimtsz given a value greater than 0, dimension lines can extend past the extension lines by the amount specified in Dimdle (*d*imension *l*ine *e*xtension). This amount is not adjusted by Dimscale. The default value is 0.
Dimdli	1.4	Sets the distance at which dimension lines are offset when you use the Baseline or Continue dimension subcommands (*d*imension *l*ine *i*ncrement). The default is 0.38 units.
Dimexe	1.4	Sets the distance the extension lines are drawn past the dimension lines (*e*xtension line *e*xtension). The default value is 0.18 units.
Dimexo	1.4	Sets the distance between the beginning of the extension line and the actual point selected at the *Extension line origin* prompt (*e*xtension line *o*ffset). The default value is 0.0625 units.
Dimlfac	2.5	Sets the global scale factor for dimension values (*l*ength *fac*tor). Linear distances will be multiplied by the value held by Dimlfac. This multiple will be entered as the dimension text. The default value is 1.0. This can be useful when drawings are not drawn to scale.

Table 3: The dimension variables (cont'd)

Variable	Version Introduced	Description
Dimlim	1.4	When set to on, dimension text is entered as two values representing a dimension range rather than a single value. The range is determined by the values given to Dimtp (*p*lus tolerance) and Dimtm (*m*inus *t*olerance). The default value is off.
Dimpost	2.6	Automatically appends text strings to dimension text. For example, if Dimpost is given the value "inches," dimension text will appear as ***value*** inches instead of just ***value.*** The default value is null. To change a previously set value to null, enter a period for the Dimpost new value. If you use Dimpost in conjunction with appended dimension text (see **Common Options/ Appending Dimension Text**), the Dimpost value is included as part of the default dimension text.
Dimrnd	2.5	Sets the amount to which all dimensions are rounded. For example, if you set Dimrnd to 1, all dimensions will be integer values. The number of decimal places affected depends on the precision value set by the Units command. The default is 0.

Table 3: The dimension variables (cont'd)

Variable	Version Introduced	Description
Dimsah	10	When set to on, allows the separate arrow blocks, Dimblk1 and Dimblk2, to replace the standard AutoCAD arrows (*separate arrow heads*). If Dimtsz is set to a value greater than 0, Dimsah has no effect.
Dimscale	1.4	Sets the scale factor for dimension variables that control dimension lines and arrows and text size (unless current text style has a fixed height). If your drawing is not full scale, you should set this variable to reflect the drawing scale. For example, for a drawing whose scale is ¼" equals 1', you should set Dimscale to 48. The default value is 1.0.
Dimse1	1.4	When set to on, the first dimension line extension is not drawn (*suppress extension 1*). The default is off.
Dimse2	1.4	When set to on, the second dimension line extension is not drawn (*suppress extension 2*). The default is off.
Dimsho	2.6	When set to on, dimension text in associative dimensions will dynamically change to reflect the location of a dimension point as it is being moved (*show dimension*). The default is off.

Table 3: The dimension variables (cont'd)

Variable	Version Introduced	Description
Dimsoxd	10	When set to on, dimension lines do not appear outside of the extension lines (*s*uppress *o*utside *e*xtension *d*imension lines). If Dimtix is also set to on and the space between the extension lines prohibits the display of a dimension line, no dimension line is drawn. The default is off.
Dimtad	1.4	When set to on and Dimtih is off, dimension text in linear dimensions will be placed above the dimension line (*t*ext *a*bove *d*imension line). When off, the dimension line will be split in two and text will be placed in line with the dimension line. The default value is off.
Dimtih	1.4	When set to on, dimension text placed between extension lines will always be horizontal (*t*ext *i*nside *h*orizontal). When set to off, text will be aligned with the dimension line. The default value is on.
Dimtix	10	When set to on, dimension text will always be placed between extension lines (*t*ext *i*nside *e*xtension). The default value is off.
Dimtm	1.4	When Dimtol or Dimlin is on, Dimtm determines the minus tolerance value of the dimension text (*t*olerance *m*inus).

Table 3: The dimension variables (cont'd)

Variable	Version Introduced	Description
Dimtofl	10	With Dimtofl on, a dimension line is always drawn between extension lines even when text is drawn outside (*text outside—forced line*). The default is off.
Dimtoh	1.4	With Dimtoh on, dimension text placed outside extension lines will always be horizontal (*text outside—horizontal*). When set to off, text outside extension lines will be aligned with the dimension line. The default is on.
Dimtol	1.4	With Dimtol on, tolerance values set by Dimtp and Dimtm are appended to the dimension text (*tolerance*). The default is off.
Dimtp	1.4	When Dimtol or Dimlim is on, Dimtp determines the plus tolerance value of the dimension text (*tolerance plus*).
Dimtsz	2.0	Sets the size of tick marks drawn in place of the standard AutoCAD arrows (*tick size*). When set to 0, the standard arrow is drawn. When greater than 0, tick marks are drawn and take precedence over Dimblk1 and Dimblk2. The default value is 0.

Table 3: The dimension variables (cont'd)

Variable	Version Introduced	Description
Dimtvp	10	When Dimtad is off, Dimtvp allows you to specify the location of the dimension text in relation to the dimension line (*t*ext *v*ertical *p*osition). A positive value places the text above the dimension line while a negative value places the text below the dimension line. The dimension line will split to accommodate the text unless the Dimtvp value is greater than 1.
Dimtxt	1.4	Sets the height of dimension text when the current text style height is set to 0. The default value is 0.18.
Dimzin	2.5	Determines the display of inches when Architectural units are used. Set to 0, zero feet or zero inches will not be displayed. Set to 1, zero feet and zero inches will be displayed. Set to 2, zero inches will not be displayed. Set to 3, zero feet will not be displayed.

location, tolerance specifications, arrow styles and sizes, and much more.

You can enter these commands at the **Dim** prompt or pick them from the Dim/Dim Vars menu. Since they are actually system variables, you can also set them using the Setvar command.

Dimensioning and Drawing Scales

Take care when dimensioning drawings at a scale other than 1:1. If the Dimscale dimension variable (see Dim Vars) is not set properly, arrows and text will appear too small or too large. In extreme cases, they may not appear at all. If you enter a dimension and arrows or text do not appear, check the Dimscale setting and make sure it is a value equal to the drawing scale.

Starting the Dimensioning Process

To add dimension labels to a drawing, select Dim from the root menu or enter Dim or Dim1 at the **Command** prompt. At this point, the prompt changes to **Dim** and you can enter any dimensioning subcommand. These and the transparent commands are the only AutoCAD commands you can enter while in the dimensioning mode.

When you are done entering dimensions under the Dim command, issue the Exit command or press **Ctrl-C** to return to the standard AutoCAD prompt. If you want to enter only a single dimension, use Dim1. This form of the command, introduced in version 2.5, returns you to the **Command** prompt automatically after you enter one dimension.

You can invoke any one of the dimension commands by entering its first three letters. For example, you can enter **Dia** instead of **Diameter**.

See Also   System Variables: Dimaso, Dimscale

DIMSTYLE (DIM)

- **VERSIONS**   11

● **PURPOSE**   Finds the current dimension style.

Sequence of Steps

•   From the keyboard: **Dimstyle** ↵

•   From the screen menu: **Dim-Dimstyle**

The current dimension style appears on the prompt line.

See Also   Restore, Save

DIR

● **VERSIONS**   2.1 and later

● **PURPOSE**   Displays a list of the files in any specified drive or
directory. If you give no specifications, you will get a list of the current drive.

Sequence of Steps

•   From the keyboard: **Dir** ↵

•   From the screen menu: **Utility-External Command-Dir**

Then complete the following step:

File specification: Enter standard DOS file names; drive letters, directory names, wildcard characters, and DOS command
switches such as /P and /W are accepted.

See Also   Catalog, Files

DIST

- **VERSIONS**   All versions

- **PURPOSE**   Gives the distance between two points in two-dimensional or three-dimensional space. It also gives the angle in the current X-Y plane, angle *from* the current X-Y plane, and the distance in X, Y, and Z coordinate values.

To Find the Distance between Two Points

- From the keyboard: **Dist** ↵

- From the screen menu: **Inquiry-Dist**

- From the pull-down menu: **Utility-Distance** (11)

Then follow these steps:

1. **First point:** Pick the beginning point of the distance.

2. **Second point:** Pick the end point of the distance.

DIVIDE

- **VERSIONS**   2.5 and later

- **PURPOSE**   Marks an object into equal divisions. You specify the number of divisions, and AutoCAD marks the object into equal parts.

To Divide an Object

- From the keyboard: **Divide** ⌐
- From the screen menu: **Edit-Divide**
- From the pull-down menu: **Modify-Divide** (11)

Then follow these steps:

1. **Select object to divide:** Pick a single object.

2. **<Number of segments>/Block:** Enter the number of segments to be marked or enter the name of the block to use
   for marking.

● OPTIONS

Block   Allows you to use an existing block as a marking device.
You receive the prompt **Block name to insert** and are asked
whether you want to align the block with the object.

If you respond **Y** to the **Align block with object** prompt, the block
will be aligned either along the axis of a line or tangent to a selected
polyline, circle, or arc. The Block option is useful for drawing a
series of objects that are equally spaced along a curved path.

● NOTES   By default, Divide uses a point entity as a marker.
Often, a point is difficult to see when placed over a line or arc. You
can set the Pdmode system variable to change the appearance of the
points, or you can use the Block option.

Version 11 can preset the number of segments and block names.
Pick **Divide Units** or **D/M Block Name** from the Options pull-
down menu. With these options preset, AutoCAD skips the prompt
for the number of segments (see step 2) and divides the selected object whenever you select **Divide** from the Modify pull-down menu.

See Also   Commands: Block, Measure, Point. System Variables:
Pmode, Pdsize

DLINE (AUTOLISP)

- **VERSIONS** 11

- **PURPOSE** Draws double lines and arcs along a path. This is handy for drawing walls in a floor plan.

Sequence of Steps

- From the keyboard: **(load "<drive>:/path/Dline")↵ dline↵**

- From the screen menu: **Bonus-Dline**

Then complete the following step:

Break/Caps/Dragline/Offset/Snap/Undo/Width/<start point>: Enter the desired option or pick the beginning point for the double line.

- **OPTIONS**

Break   Prompts you to break an existing line at the beginning and end of a double line:

Break Dlines at start and end points? OFF/<ON>:

With break on, any line for which you use the snap option at the beginning or end of a Dline will be broken between the double lines. This automatically joins two double lines in a tee-shaped intersection.

Caps   Specifies whether or not to cap either or both endpoints of the double line. An Auto option caps a double line at the end that is not located using the snap option.

Dragline   Specifies where the double lines appear relative to the points you pick: to the left, right, or centered. It also specifies the width of the double line.

Offset   Locates the beginning of a double line relative to another existing location, such as the corner of a room. The following prompts are as follows:

Offset from:
Offset toward:
Enter the offset distance:

Snap   Begins or ends a double line by snapping to an existing object. Snap controls the range in pixels to which objects will be snapped.

Undo   Backs up a line segment, much like the U option under the Line command.

Width   Controls the width of the double line.

Arc   Draws double arcs. The arc prompt changes to offer a line option, allowing you to return to drawing straight double lines.

Close   Closes a series of double line segments, much like the close option under the Line command.

See Also   AutoLISP, Osnap

DONUT

● **VERSIONS**   2.5 and later

● **PURPOSE**   Draws a circle whose line thickness you specify by entering its inside and outside diameters (see Figure 8). To create a solid dot enter 0 at the **Inside diameter** prompt. The most recent diameters are entered default values for the inside and outside diameter. Once you issue the Donut command and answer the prompts, you can place as many donuts as you like. Press ↵ to terminate the command.

To Create a Donut

- From the keyboard: **Donut** or **Doughnut** ⏎

- From the screen menu: **Draw-Donut**

- From the pull-down menu: **Draw-Donut** (11)

Then follow these steps:

1. **Inside diameter <current default>:** Enter the inside diameter of the donut.

2. **Outside diameter <current default>:** Enter the outside diameter of the donut.

3. **Center of donut:** Pick a point for the center of the donut.

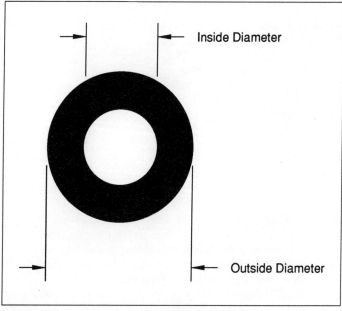

Figure 8: Inside and outside diameters of a donut

• **NOTES**   Because donuts are actually polylines, you can edit them with the Pedit command.

See Also   Fill, Pedit

DRAGMODE

• **VERSIONS**   2.0 and later

• **PURPOSE**   Controls when the Drag facility is used. The default, Auto, lets you temporarily reposition selected objects by moving them with your cursor.

To Drag an Object

•   From the keyboard: **Dragmode** ↵

•   From the screen menu: **Settings-Dragmode**

Then complete the following step:

ON/OFF/Auto <current setting>: Enter the setting.

• **OPTIONS**

ON   Enables the Drag mode, so that objects will be dragged whenever you issue the Drag command modifier.

OFF   Disables the Drag mode, so that no dragging can occur.

Auto   Causes all commands that allow dragging to automatically drag objects, whether or not you issue the Drag command modifier.

• **NOTES**   When you are editing large sets of objects, the Drag function can slow you down. It takes time for AutoCAD to refresh a temporary image, especially a complex one. If you set Dragmode on, you can use the Drag function when appropriate and dispense with it when editing large groups of objects.

See Also   Drag

DTEXT/TEXT

● **VERSIONS**   2.5 and later for Dtext, all versions for Text

● **PURPOSE** .   Allows you to enter several lines of text at once. It also displays the text on the drawing area as you type. At the first prompt, you can set the justification or set the current text style. Using either the Fit or Align options, you can tell AutoCAD to fit the text between two points.

To Enter Text Using Dtext

- From the keyboard: **Dtext** ↵ or **Text** ↵

- From the screen menu: **Draw-Dtext or Draw-next-Text**

- From the pull-down menu: **Draw-Dtext**

Then follow these steps:

1. **Justify/Style/<Start point>:** Enter the desired options or pick a start point for your text.

If you pick a point to indicate the beginning location of your text, you get the following prompts:

2. **Height <default height>:** Enter the desired text height or press ↵ to accept the default. This prompt only appears if the current style has its height set to 0.

3. **Rotation angle <default angle>:** Enter a rotation angle or press ↵ to accept the default.

4. Text: Enter the desired text.

These prompts also appear after you have selected a style or set the justification option.

● OPTIONS

Start point   Lets you indicate the location of your text. The text is automatically left-justified.

Justify   Specifies the justification of text. The prompt is:

Align/Fit/Center/Middle/Right/TL/TC/TR/ML/MC/MR/BL/ BC/BR:

This option is available only in version 11. Earlier versions display the Align/Fit/Center/Middle/Right options under the first prompt shown in step 2.

TL/TC/TR/ML/MC/MR/BL/BC/BR   Sets the justification based on the top, middle, and bottom of the text. For example, TL stands for top left and MC stands for middle center.

Align   Forces resizing of text to fit between two points. You are prompted to select the two points. The text height is scaled in proportion to its width.

Center   Centers text on the start point, which also defines the baseline of the text.

Fit   Forces text to fit between two points. Unlike Align, Fit keeps the default height and either stretches or compresses the text to fit.

Middle   Centers text at the start point. The start point is also in the middle of the text height.

Right   Right-justifies the text. The start point is on the right side of the text.

Style   Allows a new text style. The style you enter becomes the current style.

⏎   Pressing ⏎ at the first prompt if no option has been selected, highlights the most recently entered line of text. The **Text** prompt appears, allowing you to continue to add text just below that line. The current text style and angle are assumed, as is the justification setting of the most recently entered text.

● **NOTES** If you use Dtext, a box appears showing the approximate size of the text. The text appears on your drawing as you type and the box moves along as a cursor. When you press ↵, the box moves down one line. You can also pick a point anywhere on the screen for the next line of text, and still backspace all the way to the beginning line to make corrections.

If you choose a justification option other than Left, the effects will not be seen until you finish entering the text.

The Text command works much like Dtext; however, it does not display the text on your drawing as you type. The text you enter appears only in the **Command** prompt area. Also, once you press ↵, the text appears on the drawing and you are returned to the **Command** prompt. You must press ↵ twice to enter multiple lines of text.

Version 11 users can preset many Dtext options by picking **Dtext Options** from the Options pull-down menu. AutoCAD then skips the options prompt (steps 2 through 4 in the sequence of steps) and lets you go directly to text entry when you issue the Dtext command from the Draw pull-down menu.

Dtext does not work with Script files.

See Also Change, Chtext (AutoLISP), Color, Ptext (AutoLISP), Style. System Variables: Texteval, Textsize, Textstyle

DVIEW

● **VERSIONS** 10

● **PURPOSE** Displays your drawing in perspective and enables you to clip a portion of a view. Unlike the standard Zoom and Pan commands, Dview allows you to perform zooms and pans on perspective views.

To Display a Drawing with DView

- From the keyboard: **Dview** ↵

- From the screen menu: **Display-Dview**

- From the pull-down menu: **Display-Dview** (10, 11)

Then follow these steps:

1. **Select object:** Pick the objects that will help set up your perspective view.

2. **CAmera/TArget/Distance/Points/PAn/Zoom/TWist/ CLip/Hide/Off/Undo/<eXit>:** Select option from the menu or enter the capitalized letter(s) of the desired option.

The prompts you receive depend on the option selected. Once the option is completed, you are returned to the **Dview** prompt.

• OPTIONS

CAmera   Allows you to move the camera location as if you were moving a camera around, while continually aiming at the target point. CAmera prompts you for the vertical and horizontal angles of view. At each prompt, you can either enter a value or select the view by using a slide bar (on the right for vertical, on the top for horizontal). If you enter a value, it will be interpreted in relation to the current UCS (see Figure 9).

TArget   Allows you to move the target location, as if you were pointing a camera in different directions while keeping the camera location the same. TArget prompts you for the vertical and horizontal angles of view. At each prompt, you can either enter a value or select the view by using a slide bar (on the right for vertical, at the top for horizontal). See Figure 10.

Distance   Turns on the Perspective mode and allows you to set the distance from the target to the camera, as if you were moving a camera toward or away from the target point. At the prompt, enter a new distance or move the slide bar at the top of the screen to drag the three-dimensional image into the desired position (see Figure 11).

POints   Sets the target and camera points at the same time. The points you pick are in relation to the current UCS. At the prompt, pick a point for the target, then for your camera location.

PAn   Moves your camera and target point together, as if you were pointing a camera out the side window of a moving car. You cannot use the standard Pan command while viewing a drawing in perspective. See Pan for more information.

Zoom   Zooms in and out when you are viewing a drawing in parallel projection. Provides the lens focal length when you are

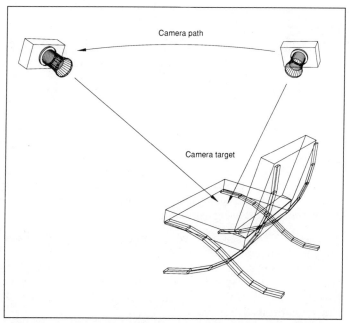

Figure 9: The CAmera option controls the camera location relative to the target

viewing a drawing in perspective. You cannot use the standard Zoom command while viewing a drawing in perspective.

If your three-dimensional view is a parallel projection, enter a new scale factor or use the slide bar at the top of the screen to visually adjust the scale factor at the **Dview/Zoom** prompt. If your three-dimensional view is a perspective, enter a new lens length value or use the slide bar at the top of the screen to determine the new lens length at the **Dview/Zoom** prompt. If you use the slide bar to adjust the focal length, the coordinate readout on the status line will dynamically display the focal length value.

Twist   Rotates the camera about the camera's line of sight, as if you were rotating the view in a camera frame. At the **Dview/Twist** prompt, enter an angle or use the cursor to visually twist the

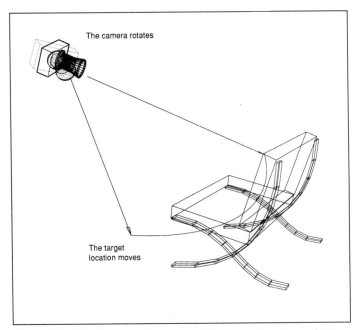

Figure 10: The TArget option controls the target location relative to the camera

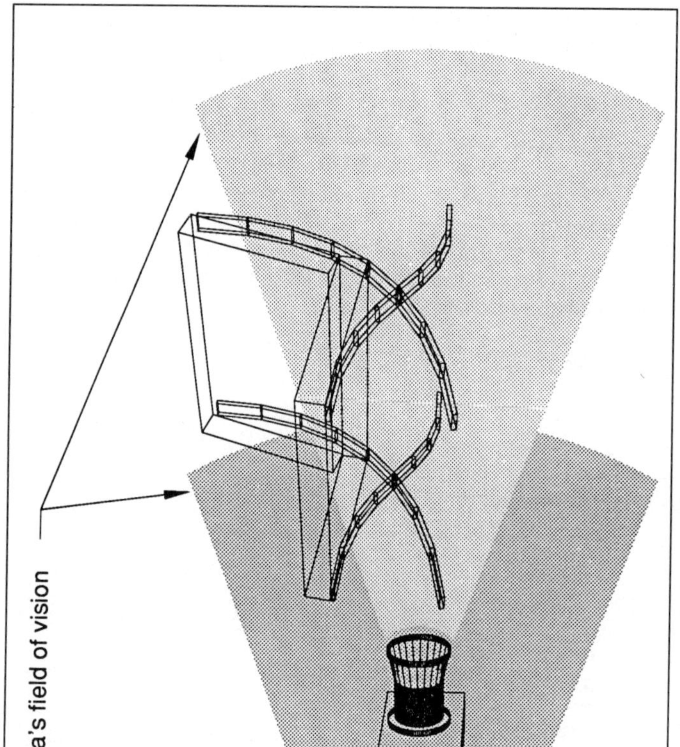

The camera's field of vision

Figure 11: The Distance option controls the distance between the camera and the target

camera view. If you use the cursor, the coordinate readout on the status line dynamically displays the camera twist angle.

CLip   Hides portions of a three-dimensional view. For example, it removes foreground objects that may interfere with a view of the background (see Figure 12). CLip displays the following prompt:

Back/Front/<Off>:

Enter **B** to set Back Clip Plane, **F** to set Front Clip Plane, or **O** or ↵ to turn off the Clip Plane function. If you select Back or Front, a prompt allows you to turn the selected clip plane on or off, or to set a distance to the clip plane. You can use the slide bar at the top of the screen to visually determine the location of the clip plane or enter a distance value. A positive value places the clip plane in front of the target point, while a negative number places it behind the target point.

Hide   Removes hidden lines from the objects displayed, turning a wire-frame view into a planar view.

eXit   Returns you to the AutoCAD **Command** prompt. Any operation you performed while in the **Dview** command prompt will affect the entire drawing, not just the selected objects.

• **NOTES**   Because a large drawing slows down the drag function, you are prompted to select objects for dragging at the beginning of the Dview command. This limits the number of objects to be dragged. You should select objects that give the general outline of your drawing as well as enough detail to indicate the drawing's orientation. If you do not pick any objects, a default three-dimensional image appears to help you select a view. You can create your own block image and use that as the default. The block should be named Dviewblock.

See Also   UCS. System Variables: Backz, Frontz, Lenslength, Target, Viewctr, Viewdir, Viewmode, Viewsize, Viewtwist

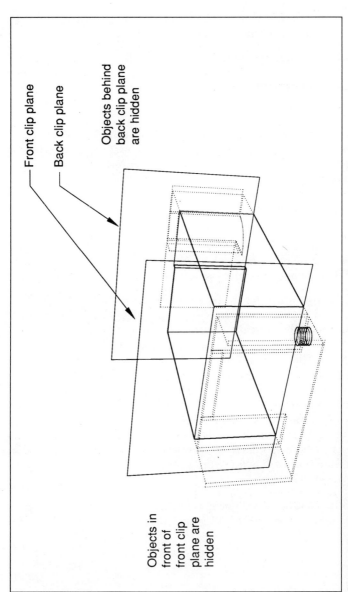

Front clip plane

Back clip plane

Objects behind
back clip plane
are hidden

Objects in
front of
front clip
plane are
hidden

Figure 12: The CLip option allows you to hide foreground or background portions of your drawing

DXBIN

● **VERSIONS**   2.1 and later

● **PURPOSE**   Imports files in the DXB file format. DXB is a binary file format that contains a limited amount of drawing information. It is the main format used by AutoShade to export files to AutoCAD.

To Import a DXB File

- From the keyboard: **Dxbin** ↵

- From the screen menu: **Utility-DXF/DXB-Dxbin**

- From the pull-down menu: **File-Exchange-DXB in** (11)

Then complete the following step:

In version 11, the Files dialog box appears. Earlier versions display the following prompt:

DXB file: Enter the name of the DXB file to import.

● **NOTES**   You can use Dxbin to convert AutoCAD three-dimensional views, both perspective and orthogonal, into two-dimensional drawings. Dxbin configures AutoCAD's plotter option to an ADI plotter that produces DXB files. This allows you to generate DXB plot files of any three-dimensional view and import these files into AutoCAD as two-dimensional images. PageMaker accepts DXB files.

See Also   Dxfin, Dxfout

DXFIN

● **VERSIONS**   All versions

● **PURPOSE**   Imports drawing files in the AutoCAD DXF format. These are ASCII files with the extension .DXF. They contain a code that allows AutoCAD to import complete drawing information. Many microcomputer and minicomputer CADD programs have a DXF converter so that you can export files to AutoCAD.

To Import a DXF File

- From the keyboard: **Dxfin** ↵

- From the screen menu: **Utility-DXF/DXB-Dxfin**

- From the pull-down menu: **File-Exchange-DXF in** (11)

Then complete the following step:

In version 11, the files dialog box appears. Earlier versions display the following prompt: **File name <current file name>:** Enter the name of the DXF file to import.

● **NOTES**   To import a DXF file, open a new file that does not contain any nameable variable definitions such as layers, line types, text styles, and views. Then, issue the Dxfin command. (If the current file already contains nameable variables, only the drawn objects in the imported file are imported. Line types, layers, and so on are not imported.) When you enter the name of the DXF file you wish to import, do not include the .DXF extension.

See Also   Dxfout, Dxbin

DXFOUT

● **VERSIONS**   All versions

● **PURPOSE**   Creates a copy of your current file in the DXF file format for export to other programs. It can also create a binary version of the DXF format, which is highly compressed compared with the ASCII version.

To Export a DXF File

- From the keyboard: **Dxfout** ⏎

- From the screen menu: **Utility-DXF/DXB-Dxfout**

- From the pull-down menu: **File-Exchange-DXF out** (11)

Then follow these steps:

In version 11, the files dialog box appears. Earlier versions display the following prompts:

1. **File name <default current file name>:** Enter the file name or press ⏎ for default.

2. **Enter decimal places of accuracy (0 to 16) /Entities/Binary <6>:** Enter a value representing the decimal place accuracy of your DXF file or press ⏎ to accept the default (6).

● **OPTIONS**

(0 to 16)   Controls the decimal accuracy of the DXF file to be created. The default value is 6.

Entities   Allows you to select specific objects or a portion of the current drawing to be exported. You are then prompted to select objects.

Binary Creates a binary version of the DXF file, also with the .DXF extension. Do not confuse this with the DXB file format.

● **NOTES** Many programs use DXF files. Some are converters that translate DXF files for desktop publishing programs, paint programs, or other CADD programs. There are even programs that use DXF files for analysis or for generating database information.

See Also Commands: Dxbin, Dxfin

EDGE (AUTOLISP)

● **VERSIONS** 10 and later

● **PURPOSE** Turns the visibility of a 3Dface edge on or off.

To Load the Edge Command

- From the keyboard: (**load "<drive>:/path/edge"**)↵ **edge** ↵

- From the screen menu: **Bonus-Edge** (11)

Then complete the following step:

Display/<Select edge>: Pick a 3dface edge to make it invisible or enter **D** to highlight an invisible edge.

● **NOTES** You can select only visible edges. To make an edge visible, use the Display option.

From the keyboard, you have to load Edge only once per editing session. You can then use Edge at any time. It is not necessary to load Edge if you are using the menu.

See Also Splframe

EDGESURF

● **VERSIONS**   10, 11

● **PURPOSE**   Edgesurf draws a three-dimensional surface based on four objects. These objects can be lines, arcs, polylines, or three-dimensional polylines, but they must join exactly end-to-end.

To Create a 3D Surface Using Edgesurf

- From the keyboard: **Edgesurf** ↵

- From the screen menu: **3D-Edgesurf** (10), **Draw-next-3D surfs-Edgesurf** (11)

- From the pull-down menu: **Draw-3D Construction-Edge Defined Surface Patch** (10), **Draw-Surfaces-Edge Defined Surface Patch** (11)

Then follow these steps:

1. **Select edge 1:** Pick the first object defining an edge.

2. **Select edge 2:** Pick the second object defining an edge.

3. **Select edge 3:** Pick the third object defining an edge.

4. **Select edge 4:** Pick the fourth object defining an edge.

● **NOTES**   The type of surface drawn by Edgesurf is called a *Coons surface patch* (see Figure 13).

The first edge selected defines the M direction of the mesh, and the edges adjoining the first define the N direction. The end point closest to the point selected becomes the origin of the M and N directions.

The Surftab1 and Surftab2 system variables control the number of facets in the M and N directions, respectively. Increasing the number of facets gives a smoother mesh, but increases the file size of the

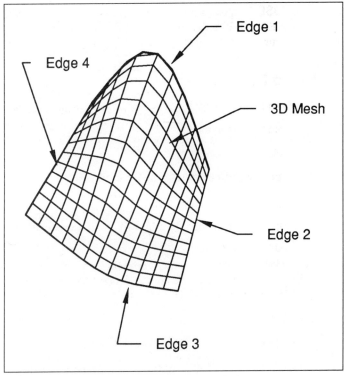

Figure 13: A Coons surface patch

drawing considerably. This increases file-opening, redrawing, and regeneration times. See Setvar for details.

See Also   Commands: Pedit. System Variables: Surftab1, Surftab2

EDIT

• **VERSIONS**   2.5 and later

● **PURPOSE**   Opens a specified text file in the DOS EDLIN line editor. The EDLIN.COM file must be in the default drive and directory. See your DOS manual for details on EDLIN.

To Edit a Text File

*   From the keyboard: **Edit** ↵

*   From the screen menu: **Utility-External Command-Edit**

Then complete the following step:

File to edit: Enter the DOS or ASCII file name.

● **NOTES**   Use this command to create an ASCII file for the Attext or Script commands.

You can edit the Acad.pgp to start a different text editor within AutoCAD (see Acad.pgp).

See Also   Attext, EDLIN (in your DOS manual), Script

EDIT AN EXISTING DRAWING

● **VERSIONS**   All versions

● **PURPOSE**   Opens an existing file from the main menu.

Sequence of Steps

*   At the main menu: Press **2** ↵

*   From the DOS prompt: **ACAD <filename>**↵ **2**↵↵

Then complete the following step:

Enter NAME of drawing <default>: Enter the name of an existing drawing, including the drive and path name if different from the current setting, or press ⏎ to accept the default name.

● **NOTES**   You can automatically load a drawing file using a script file. Include **2** as the first item in the script, followed by a single blank line.

To both load a file and launch a script from the DOS prompt, type **acad**, a space, the drawing file name, a space, and the script file name, as follows:

   acad <filename> <script>

See Also   Commands: Script

ELEV

● **VERSIONS**   2.0 and later

● **PURPOSE**   The Elev command allows you to set the default Z-axis elevation and thickness of objects being drawn. Normally, objects will be placed at a 0 elevation. Once you enter an elevation or thickness with the Elev command, all objects will be given the selected option value. Objects you drew before using the Elev command are not affected. You can also change the elevation of an existing object with the Move command.

To Set Elevation and Thickness

- From the keyboard: **Elev** ⏎

- From the screen menu: **Settings-Elev**

Then follow these steps:

1.   **New current elevation <current default>: <elevation>**

2.   **New current thickness <current default>: <thickness>**

● **OPTIONS**

New current elevation   Sets the current default elevation in the
Z-axis.

New current thickness   Sets the current default thickness in the
Z-axis.

See Also   Commands: Ddemodes, Move. System Variables:
Elevation

ELLIPSE

● **VERSIONS**   2.5 and later

● **PURPOSE**   Draws an ellipse for which you specify the major
and minor axes, a center point and two axis points, or the center point
and radius or diameter of an isometric circle. It also allows you to
define a second projection of a three-dimensional circle through the
Rotation option.

To Draw an Ellipse

●   From the keyboard: **Ellipse** ↵

●   From the screen menu: **Draw-Ellipse**

●   From the pull-down menu: **Draw-Ellipse** (11)

Then complete the following step:

> **<Axis endpoint 1>/Center:** Pick a point defining one end of the ellipse or enter **C** to enter the center point.

If you select the default option by picking a point, the following prompts appear:

> **Axis endpoint 2:** Pick a point defining the opposite end of the ellipse.

> **<Other axis distance>/Rotation:** Pick a point defining the other axis of the ellipse or enter **R** to enter a rotation value.

● OPTIONS

Center   Allows you to pick the ellipse center point.

Axis endpoint   Allows you to enter the endpoint of one of the ellipse's axes (see Figure 14).

Other axis distance   Appears after you have already defined one of the ellipse's axes. Enter the distance from the center of the ellipse to the second axis endpoint (see Figure 14).

Isocircle   Appears if the current snap mode is set to Isometric. This option prompts you to select a center and diameter or radius for the ellipse. AutoCAD draws an isometric circle based on the current Isoplane setting.

Rotation   Allows you to enter an ellipse rotation value. Imagine the ellipse to be a two-dimensional projection of a three-dimensional circle rotated on an axis. As the circle is rotated, it appears to turn into an ellipse. The rotation value determines the rotation angle of this circle. A 0-degree value displays a full circle; an 80-degree value displays a narrow ellipse (see Figure 15).

● NOTES
Because an ellipse is actually a polyline, you can edit it using the Pedit command.

See Also   Commands: Isoplane, Snap/Style

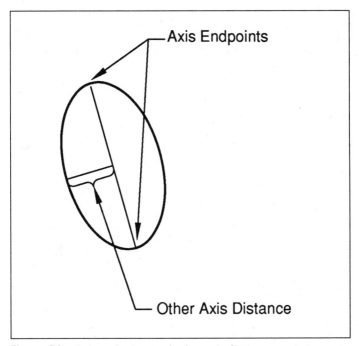

Figure 14: Axis endpoints and other axis distance

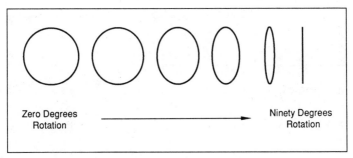

Figure 15: A rotated ellipse

END

● **VERSIONS** All versions

● **PURPOSE** Simultaneously exits and saves a file. Edits made prior to the End command are saved.

Sequence of Steps

- From the keyboard: **End** ↵
- From the screen menu: **Utility-End-Yes**
- From the pull-down menu: **File-End**

● **NOTES** You can also use the End AutoLISP utility from the Bonus menu of version 11. This utility compresses your file by issuing the Save and Quit commands in sequence, then prompts for confirmation that you want to exit the file.

See Also Quit, Save

ERASE

● **VERSIONS** All versions

● **PURPOSE** Erases one or several objects from the drawing, selected using the standard options.

To Erase Objects

- From the keyboard: **Erase** ↵
- From the screen menu: **Edit-Erase**

- From the pull-down menu: **Edit-Erase** (9), **Modify-Erase** (10, 11)

Then complete the following step:

Select objects: Select the objects to be erased.

● NOTES   To erase an object that is overlapped by another, use a crossing window to select both objects, then use the Remove selection option and remove the object on top from the selection set with a single pick.

See Also   Commands: Auto, Multiple, Oops, Select-Si

EXIT (DIM)

● VERSIONS   1.4 and later

● PURPOSE   Exits Dim command and returns you to the standard **Command** prompt.

To Exit from Dim

- From the keyboard: **Exit** ↵

- From the screen menu: **Dim-Exit**

● NOTES   You can press **Ctrl-C** or type **Exi** in place of Exit. If you entered Dim1 to begin dimensioning, Exit is not needed.

EXIT AUTOCAD

● VERSIONS   All versions

• **PURPOSE**   Ends the AutoCAD session and returns to the DOS prompt.

To Exit AutoCAD

•   At the main menu: **0** ↵

See Also   Commands: Quit, End

EXPLODE

• **VERSIONS**   2.5 and later

• **PURPOSE**   Reduces a block, polyline, associative dimension, or three-dimensional mesh to its component objects. If a block is nested, Explode only "unblocks" the outermost block.

To Explode an Object

•   From the keyboard: **Explode** ↵

•   From the screen menu: **Edit-Explode**

Then complete the following step:

Select block reference, polyline, dimension, or mesh: Select the object to be exploded.

• **NOTES**   Blocks inserted with Minsert and blocks with unequal X, Y, or Z insertion scale factors cannot be exploded.

Wide polylines lose their width properties when exploded.

See Also   Command: Undo, Xplode

EXTEND

- **VERSIONS**   2.5 and later

- **PURPOSE**   Lengthens an object to meet another object.

To Extend an Object

- From the keyboard: **Extend** ⏎

- From the screen menu: **Edit-Extend**

- From the pull-down menu: **Edit-Extend** (9), **Modify-Extend** (10, 11)

Then follow these steps:

1. **Select boundary edge(s)**... Pick one or more objects to which to extend other objects.

2. **<Select objects to extend>/Undo:** Select objects to be extended one at a time or enter **U** to undo the last extend operation.

For versions prior to 11, step 2 shows only the **Select objects** prompt.

- **NOTES**   You cannot extend objects within blocks or use blocks as boundary edges. Also, boundary edges must be in the path of the objects to be extended.

You can only extend objects that lie in a plane parallel to the current user coordinate system (UCS).

If you are not viewing the current UCS in plan, you may get an erroneous result. It is best to use the Plan command to view the current UCS in plan, and then proceed with the Extend command.

At times, objects will not extend properly even when all conditions are met. If this problem occurs, use the Zoom or Pan command to change your view, then reissue the Extend command.

See Also   Change, Trim

FACT (AUTOLISP)

- **VERSIONS**   9 and later

- **PURPOSE**   Finds the factorial of an integer.

Sequence of Steps

- From the keyboard: (**load "<drive>:/path/fact"**) ↵ **fact** ↵
- From the screen menu: **Bonus-Fact** (11)

Then complete the following step:

Enter an integer: Enter the integer for which you want to find the factorial.

- **NOTES**   This AutoLISP program demonstrates AutoLISP's ability to perform recursions.

From the keyboard, you have to load Edge only once per editing session. You can then use Edge at any time. It is not necessary to load Edge if you are using the menu.

See Also   AutoLISP

FILES DIALOG BOX

● **VERSIONS** 11

● **PURPOSE** In version 11, the files dialog box appears when you use any command that reads or creates external files. These commands are Attext, Dxbin, Dxfin, Dxfout, Filmroll, Igesin, Igesout, Linetype, Load, Menu, Mslide, Save, Script, Style, Vslide, and Wblock.

● **OPTIONS**

The following input boxes appear in the Files dialog box:

Directory Lets you enter the name of a directory in which to place your file.

Pattern Lets you specify the type of file you want displayed in the list of files. You can use the standard DOS wildcard characters to filter file names.

File Displays the default file name to be saved. You can highlight this box and enter a new name or pick a name from the file list.

OK Tells AutoCAD to accept the name in the File box and return to the Command prompt.

Cancel Cancels the command.

Type it Closes the dialog box and returns to the file name prompt you normally see with earlier versions of AutoCAD.

Default Causes the name in the File box to revert to the default file name.

● **NOTES** To disable the Files dialog box display, set the Filedia system variable to **0**. You can still display the dialog box by entering a tilde (~) either at the File name prompt or with the Insert command.

For some commands, a few of the options will be disabled.

See Also System Variable: Filedia

FILES/FILE UTILITIES

● **VERSIONS** All versions

● **PURPOSE** Allows you to manipulate files on your disk without having to exit AutoCAD. You can list all or specified files, delete them, rename them, or copy them.

To Access the File Utility Menu

• From the keyboard: **Files** ↵

• From the screen menu: **Utility-Files**

• From the Main menu: **6** ↵

Then complete the following step:

If you are in the Drawing editor, the screen switches to Text mode and the File Utility Menu appears with the following options:

0. Exit File Utility Menu
1. List Drawing files
2. List user specified files
3. Delete files
4. Rename files
5. Copy file
6. Unlock files
Enter selection (0 to 5) <0>:

Enter the number corresponding to the desired option.

● OPTIONS

Exit File Utility Menu   Exits the Files command.

List Drawing files   Lists all drawing files in a directory you specify.

List user specified files   Lists files you specify in the directory you specify. Accepts wildcard specifications.

Delete files   Deletes files you specify. Accepts wildcard specifications.

Rename files   Renames files. Prompts you for the current file name, then for a new name.

Copy file   Copies files.

Unlock files   Allows access to files that have been locked due to another user's instructions or by an aborted AutoCAD session. A list is displayed showing which user locked the file and when it was locked.

● NOTES   When entering file names, you must include the file extension. For the Unlock files option, give the .DWG file name.

The File Utilities option on the opening Main menu works in the same way as the Files command.

When deleting files, take care not to delete files AutoCAD needs for its internal operation. If you or someone on your network is currently editing a file, do not delete AutoCAD temporary files with the extension .$AC, .AC$, or .$A. Table 4 lists other AutoCAD file extensions and their purposes.

See Also   External Commands

Table 4: AutoCAD files extensions and their meanings

File Description	Standard Extension	Lock File Extension
Drawing backup file	.BAK	.BKK
AutoCAD configuration file	.CFG	.CFK
Drawing file	.DWG	.DWK
Binary data exchange file	.DXB	.DBK
Drawing interchange file	.DXF	.DFK
Attribute data in DXF format	.DXX	.DXK
AutoShade filmroll file	.FLM	.FLK
IGES drawing interchange file	.IGS	.IGK
Line type definition file	.LIN	.LIK
Printer plot file	.LST	.LSK
Menu file	.MNU	.MNK
Backup of a file converted from an early version of AutoCAD	.OLD	.OLK
Plot file	.PLT	.PLK
ADI printer plot file	.PRP	.PRK
AutoCAD login file	.PWD	.PWK
Shape or Font file	.SHX	.SHK
Slide files	.SLD	.SDK

FILL

● **VERSIONS**   All versions

- **PURPOSE**   Turns on or off the solid fills of solids, traces, and polylines. When Fill is off, solid filled areas are only outlined, both on the screen and in prints.

Sequence of Steps

- From the keyboard: **Fill** ⏎

- From the screen menu: **Draw-Pline-Fill off** or **Draw-Trace-Fill off/on** or **Draw-Solid-Fill off/on**

See Also   Commands: Pline, Trace, Solid. System Variables: Fillmode

FILLET

- **VERSIONS**   All versions

- **PURPOSE**   Fillet uses an intermediate arc to join two non-parallel lines, a line and an arc, or segments of a polyline.

Sequence of Steps

- From the keyboard: **Fillet** ⏎

- From the screen menu: **Edit-next-Fillet**

- From the pull-down menu: **Modify-Fillet** (10, 11)

Then follow these steps:

1. **Polyline/Radius/<select first line>:** Pick the first line.

2. **Select second line:** Pick the second line.

● OPTIONS

Polyline   Fillets all line segments within a polyline. You are prompted to select a two-dimensional polyline. All joining polyline segments are then filleted.

Radius   Allows you to specify radius of the fillet arc.

● NOTES   In versions previous to 11, Fillet joins the end points closest to the intersection. In version 11, the location you use to pick objects determines which part of the fillet is trimmed. If the lines (or line and arc) already intersect, Fillet substitutes the specified arc for the existing corner. To connect two nonparallel lines with a corner rather than an arc, set the radius to 0.

If you are not viewing the current UCS in plan, Fillet may give you the wrong result. Use the Plan command to view the current UCS in plan before issuing the Fillet command.

See Also   Commands: Chamfer. System Variables: Filletrad

FILMROLL

● VERSIONS   9 and later

● PURPOSE   Filmroll saves to a file on disk all scenes created by the Scene Ashade AutoLISP function. The scenes are saved in a format that the AutoShade program can read.

Sequence of Steps

- From the keyboard: **Filmroll** ↵
- From the screen menu: **Ashade-Action-Filmroll**
- From the pull-down menu: **Options-Ashade-Filmroll icon** (9, 10), **Utility-Ashade-Filmroll icon** (11)

Then complete the following step:

In version 11, the Files dialog box appears. Earlier versions display the following prompts:

Enter filmroll file name <current file name>: Enter the desired file name for the filmroll.

Creating the filmroll file

Filmroll file created

GRAPHSCR/TEXTSCR

● **VERSIONS**   2.5 and later

● **PURPOSE**   Flips the screen to either graphics or text mode. This is commonly used in script files, AutoLISP programs, and menu options. When preceded by an apostrophe, these commands can be used transparently. If you have a dual-screen system, these commands are ignored.

To Flip to Graphics or Text

•   From the keyboard: 'Graphscr ↵ or 'Textscr ↵

GRID

● **VERSIONS**   All versions

● **PURPOSE**   Sets the grid spacing.

Sequence of Steps

- From the keyboard: **Grid** ↵
- From the screen menu: **Settings-Grid**

Then complete the following step:

Grid spacing(X) or ON/OFF/Snap/Aspect <default value>: Enter the desired grid spacing or other option.

● OPTIONS

Grid spacing(X)   Allows you to enter the desired grid spacing in drawing units. Enter 0 to make the grid spacing reflect the Snap setting.

ON   Turns on the grid display. The F7 key performs the same function.

OFF   Turns off the grid display. The F7 key performs the same function.

Snap   Sets the grid spacing to reflect the Snap spacing.

Aspect   Specifies a grid spacing in the Y-axis that is different from the spacing in the X-axis.

● NOTES
If you follow the grid spacing value with X at the **Grid spacing** prompt, AutoCAD interprets the value as a multiple of the Snap setting. For example, if you enter 2 at the **Grid spacing** prompt, the grid points will be spaced two units apart. If you enter 2X, the grid points will be twice as far apart as the Snap settings.

At times, a grid setting may obscure the view of your drawing. If this happens, AutoCAD automatically turns off the grid mode and displays the message **Grid too dense to display.**

If you are using multiple viewports in Paperspace, you can set the grid differently for each viewport.

See Also   Ddrmodes

HANDLES

● **VERSIONS**   10 and later

● **PURPOSE**   Enables you to access each object in a drawing by its name.

Sequence of Steps

●   From the keyboard: **Handles** ↵

The following prompts appear:

Handles are disabled
ON/DESTROY: <option> Enter the desired option.

● **OPTIONS**

ON   Enables the Handles function, giving every object drawn an alphanumeric name.

DESTROY   Disables the Handles function, destroying any currently existing handles in the drawing.

● **NOTES**   The List command displays the selected object's handle in addition to the other information List provides. If you are programming in AutoLISP, you can identify entities using the Handent AutoLISP function.

Handle information is written to DXF files and therefore can help you extract database information from a drawing.

See Also   Commands: DXFout, List, System Variables: Handles

HATCH

- **VERSIONS**   All versions

- **PURPOSE**   Fills an area defined by lines, arcs, circles, and polylines with either a predefined pattern or a simple hatch pattern.

Sequence of Steps

- From the keyboard: **Hatch** ↵

- From the screen menu: **Draw-Hatch**

- From the pull-down menu: **Draw-Hatch**

Then complete the following step:

Pattern (? or name/U,style) <default pattern>: Enter the pattern name or enter **U** to create a simple crosshatch pattern.

- **OPTIONS**

U   Defines a simple hatch pattern, including hatch angle, spacing between lines, and whether or not you want a crosshatch. Crosshatching occurs at 90 degrees to the first hatch lines.

?   Lists the names of available hatch patterns.

pattern name   Can be entered at the **Pattern** prompt. You are prompted for the scale and angle for the pattern. In general, the pattern scale should be the same as the drawing scale. The following modifiers control how the pattern is created. To use these modifiers, enter the pattern name at the **Pattern** prompt, followed by a comma and the modifier.

N   Fills each alternate area. For example, if you have four concentric circles and you pick all four circles at the **Select objects** prompt, the hatch pattern will fill in the space between the outer circle and the next circle, skip the space between the second and third circle, and fill the space between the third and fourth circle. The N option is the default.

O   Fills only the outermost area selected.

I   Causes the entire area within the objects selected to be hatched, regardless of other enclosed areas within the selected area. This option also forces the hatch pattern to avoid hatching over text.

scaleXP   When entered at the scale prompt in version 11, this modifier lets you specify a hatch scale relative to Paperspace. See Zoom/XP.

● **NOTES**   There are 53 predefined patterns, illustrated in Figure 16 (41 for versions 10 and earlier). To list these patterns, enter **Hatch?**. You can create your own hatch patterns by editing the Acad.PAT file. This file uses numeric codes to define the patterns.

The objects that define the hatch area should be joined end-to-end and be closed. If you use lines and arcs, the endpoints of the objects must meet exactly end-to-end. Polylines should be closed.

To make the hatch pattern begin at a specific point, use the Rotate option under the Snap command to set the snap origin to the desired beginning point. Hatch uses the snap origin to determine where to start the hatch pattern.

If you need to edit a hatch pattern, use the Explode command to break the pattern into its component lines.

Version 11 can preset hatch patterns, pattern scales, and rotation angles using the Hatch options on the Options pull-down menu. Then, whenever you issue Hatch from the Draw pull-down menu, you will go directly to the **Select objects** prompt, skipping over the prompts for hatch pattern, scale, and rotation.

See Also   Commands: Explode, Snap/Rotate

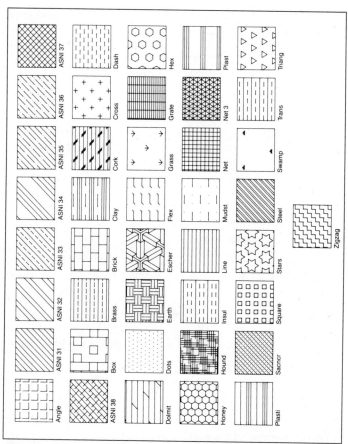

Figure 16:   The standard hatch patterns

HELP/?

- **VERSIONS**   All versions

- **PURPOSE**   Gives a brief description of how to use a particular command. Use Help in the middle of another command to get specific information about that command. Enter **Help** preceded by an apostrophe at any prompt in the command. You can use a question mark in place of the word *Help*.

To Access Help

- From the keyboard: **Help** ↵ or **'help** ↵ or **?** ↵

- From the screen menu: **Inquiry-Help**

- From the pull-down menu: **Help-Help** (9, 10), **Assist-Help!** (11)

Then complete the following step:

Command name (RETURN for list): Enter the name of the command in question or press ↵ for a list of commands and a brief description of point selection.

● **NOTES**   When Help is used in the middle of a command, version 11 users receive information related to the specific prompt being displayed.

By issuing Help at the **Command** prompt, you can get a listing of available commands and system variables, along with a description of the Select object options and coordinate input.

HIDE

● **VERSIONS**   2.1 and later

● **PURPOSE**   Removes hidden lines on an orthagonal three-dimensional view.

Sequence of Steps

- From the keyboard: **Hide** ↵

- From the screen menu: **Display-Vpoint-Hide-Yes**

- From the pull-down menu: **Display-3D View-Hide icon** (9), **Display-Vpoint-Hide icon** (10, 11)

Then complete the following step:

Removing hidden lines: <number of vectors hidden>

● **NOTES**   Once you issue Hide, the **Removing hidden lines** prompt appears, followed by a series of numbers that count off the lines as they are hidden. For complex 3D views, you may want to use Mslide to save a three-dimensional view with hidden lines removed. In a perspective view, use the Hide option under Dview.

You can also use Shade to get a quick rendering of a 3D model.

See Also   Commands: Shade

HOMETEXT (DIM)

● **VERSIONS**   2.6 and later

● **PURPOSE**   Moves the text of a dimension back to its default position after it has been moved using the Stretch command. Hometext works only with associative dimensions that have not been exploded.

To Return Dimension Text to Position

- From the keyboard: **Hometext** ↵

- From the screen menu: **Dim-next-Hometext**

Then complete the following step:

Select objects: Pick the dimensions that need text to be moved to the default position.

See Also   Dimension Variables: Dimaso

HORIZONTAL (DIM)

- **VERSIONS**   1.4 and later

- **PURPOSE**   Creates a horizontal dimension regardless of the extension line origins or the orientation of the object picked.

Before Dimensioning

You must have issued the Dim or Dim1 command to use any dimensioning subcommand.

Sequence of Steps

- From the keyboard: **Horizontal** ↵

- From the screen menu: **Dim-Linear-Horizontal**

Then follow these steps:

1. **First extension line origin or RETURN to select:** Pick one end of the object to be dimensioned.

2. **Second extension line origin:** Pick the other end of the object.

3. **Dimension line location:** Pick a point or enter a coordinate indicating the location of the dimension line.

4. **Dimension text: <default dimension>:** Press ↵ to accept the default dimensions or enter a dimension value.

ID

- **VERSIONS**   All versions

- **PURPOSE**   Displays the X, Y, and Z coordinate values of a point.

Sequence of Steps

- Keyboard: **Id** ⏎

- From the screen menu: **Inquiry-Id**

Then complete the following step:

Point: Pick a point.

- **NOTES**   A point you select with Id becomes the last point in the current editing session. You can access this point by using the at sign (@) from any point selection prompt.

IGESIN

- **VERSIONS**   2.5 and later

- **PURPOSE**   Use Igesin to import files in the IGES format.

Sequence of Steps

- From the keyboard: **Igesin** ⏎

- From the screen menu: **Utility-Iges-Igesin**

- From the pull-down menu: **File-EXCHANGE-IGES in** (11)

Then complete the following step:

In version 11, the files dialog box appears. Earlier versions display the following prompt:

File name: <IGES file names>

● **NOTES**   You can import IGES files only to a fresh, empty drawing file. You cannot add information to an existing AutoCAD file.

See Also   Command: Igesout

IGESOUT

● **VERSIONS**   2.5 and later

● **PURPOSE**   Makes a copy of your current file in the IGES format.

Sequence of Steps

* From the keyboard: **Igesout** ↵

* From the screen menu: **Utility-Iges-Igesout**

* From the pull-down menu: **Files-EXCHANGE-IGES out** (11)

Then complete the following step:

In version 11, the files dialog box appears. Earlier versions display the following prompt:

File name: <IGES file name>

See Also   Command: Igesin

INSERT

● **VERSIONS**   All versions

● **PURPOSE**   Inserts blocks contained within the current file, or other drawing files.

Sequence of Steps

- From the keyboard: **Insert** ↵

- From the screen menu: **Blocks-Insert** or **Draw-Insert**

- From the pull-down menu: **Draw-Insert** (10, 11)

Then follow these steps:

1. **Block name (or ?)<last block inserted>:** Enter the block or drawing name or, in version 11, ~ to display the File dialog box.

2. **Insertion point:** Enter a coordinate value, pick a point with cursor, or enter a preset option.

3. **X scale factor <1> / Corner / XYZ:** Enter an X scale factor, **C** for corner, **XYZ** to specify the individual X, Y, and Z scale factors, or ↵ to accept the default X scale factor of 1. If you press ↵ without entering any value or option, the prompt **Y scale factor (default=X):** appears. Enter a Y scale factor or ↵ for the default Y=X scale factor.

4. **Rotation angle <0>:** Enter the rotation angle for the block or pick a point on the screen to indicate the angle. (This last prompt does not appear if you use the Rotate preset option.)

● OPTIONS

~ (tilde)   Entered at the **Block name** prompt, causes a dialog box to appear. The dialog box lets you select external files for insertion. This option is available in version 11 only.

=   Replaces a block with an external file. See *Notes*.

X scale factor   Scales the block in the X-axis. If you enter a value, you are prompted for the Y scale factor.

Corner   Allows you to enter the X and Y scale factors simultaneously. To scale the block by a factor of 1 in the X-axis and 2 in the Y-axis, enter **C** at the **X scale factor** prompt and then enter **@1,2**. Entering a coordinate value or picking a point at the X scale factor prompt has the same effect.

XYZ   Gives individual X, Y, and Z scale factors. You will be prompted for the factors.

The following options are available at the **Insertion point** prompt. They are called insert *presets* because they allow you to preset the scale and rotation angle of a block before you select an insertion point. Once you select a preset option, the dragged image will conform to the setting used.

Scale   Allows you to enter a single scale factor for the block. This factor governs X-, Y-, and Z-axis scaling. You will not be prompted for a scale factor after you select the insertion point.

Xscale   Sets the X scale factor.

Yscale   Sets the Y scale factor.

Zscale   Sets the Z scale factor.

Rotate   Enters a rotation angle for the block. You are not prompted for rotation angle after you select the insertion point.

PScale   The same as Scale but is used only while positioning the block for insertion. You are later prompted for a scale factor.

PXscale   The same as PScale but affects only the X scale factor.

PYscale   The same as PScale but affects only the Y scale factor.

PZscale   The same as PScale but affects only the Z scale factor.

PRotate   The same as Rotate but is used only while positioning the block for insertion. You are later prompted for a rotation factor.

● **NOTES**   If a block has previously been inserted, it becomes the default block for insertion. Enter ? to see a list of the blocks in the current file. Coordinate values are in relation to the current UCS.

To insert the individual entities in a block (rather than the block as a single object), type an asterisk before its name at the **Block name** prompt. To bring the contents of an external file in as individual entities, insert the file in the normal way and use the Explode command to break it into its individual components. To insert a mirror image of a block, enter a negative value at either the X scale factor or Y scale factor prompt.

If the inserted block or file contains an attribute and the Attreq system variable is set to 1, you are prompted for the attribute information after you have entered the rotation angle. If the system variable Attdia is set to 1, a dialog box with the attribute prompts appears. The default setting for Attreq is 1. Attdia is normally set to 0.

You can also use Insert to replace or update a block with an external drawing file. For example, to replace a block Chair1 with an external file Chair2, enter **Chair1=Chair2** at the **Block name** prompt. If the block and the external file names are the same (Chair1, for example) enter **Chair1=**. Note, however, named objects in the current drawing have priority over those in an imported file.

When you attempt to replace blocks containing attributes, the old attributes will remain even though the block has been changed. The only solution is to delete the old block and then insert the new (external) block and re-enter the attribute values. You can also use the Attredef AutoLISP utility (see Attredef).

Finally, an external file will be inserted with its world coordinate system aligned with the current user coordinate system. A block will be inserted with its UCS orientation aligned with the current UCS.

See Also   Commands: Attdef, Attredef, Base, Block, Explode, Files dialog box, Xref. System Variables: Attdia, Attreq, Filedia

INSTALLATION

● **VERSIONS**   All versions

Sequence of Steps

1. For versions before 10/386, create a directory on your hard disk to store AutoCAD. Typically, the directory name used is ACAD. Copy all the contents of each disk into the ACAD directory. For versions 10–386 and later, place disk 1 in drive A and enter **type install**, then follow the directions shown on the screen.

2. You can create subdirectories called Sample, Source, Support, and Bonus for the disks with the same respective names. However, if you do this, be sure you have the following statement in your Autoexec.bat file:

   SET ACAD=C:\ACAD\SUPPORT

   This directs AutoCAD to look in drive C in the directory \ACAD\SUPPORT for the support files AutoCAD needs. These support files contain line type, hatch pattern, text definitions, and other features.

3. See *Configuring AutoCAD* for configuration information.

ISOPLANE

● **VERSIONS**   All versions

● **PURPOSE**   When the snap mode is set to the isometric style, Isoplane lets you switch the cursor orientation between the left, top, and right isometric planes.

Sequence of Steps

● From the keyboard: **Isoplane** ↵

Then follow these steps:

1. **Left/Top/Right/<Toggle>:** Enter your choice or press ↵ to go to the next isoplane.

2. **Current Isometric plane is:** Enter the new isoplane.

See Also   Commands: Ddrmodes, Snap

LAYER

● **VERSIONS**   All versions

● **PURPOSE**   Creates new layers, assigns colors and line types to layers, and sets the current layer. Layer allows you to control which layers are displayed.

Sequence of Steps

● From the keyboard: **Layer** ↵

● From the screen menu: **Layer**

● **OPTIONS**

?   Displays the list of existing layers. Wildcards are accepted.

Make   Creates a new layer and makes it current.

Set   Makes an existing layer the current layer.

New   Creates a new layer.

ON   Turns on layers.

OFF   Turns off layers.

Color   Sets color of a layer.

Ltype   Sets line type of a layer.

Freeze   Freezes one or more layers.

Thaw   Unfreezes one or more layers.

● **NOTES**   All Layer options except Make, Set, and New allow you to enter wildcard characters (question marks and asterisks) for input. For example, if you want to turn off all layers whose names begin with G, enter **G*** at the **Layers to turn off** prompt.

Freeze/Thaw and On/Off both control whether or not a layer is displayed. However, unlike Off, Freeze makes AutoCAD ignore objects on frozen layers. This allows faster regenerations. Freeze also affects blocks differently than Off.

Layer 0, the default layer when you open a new file, is white (number 7) and has continuous line type. Layer 0 also has some unique properties. If you include objects on Layer 0 in a block, they take on the color and line type of the layer on which the block is inserted. The objects must be created with the Byblock color (see Color).

The dimension layer Defpoints is also unique. When it is turned off, objects on this layer are still displayed, but will not appear on prints or plots. This makes the Defpoints layer suitable for layout lines.

See Also   Color, Ddlmodes, Linetype, Regen, Regenauto, Vplayer, Wildcards

LEADER (DIM)

● **VERSIONS**   1.4 and later

● **PURPOSE**   Adds notes with arrows to drawings.

Before Dimensioning

You must have issued the Dim or Dim1 command to use any dimensioning subcommand.

To Add Leaders

- From the keyboard: **Leader** ↵

- From the screen menu: **Dim-Leader**

Then follow these steps:

1. **Leader start:** Pick a point to start the leader. This is the point where the arrow will be placed.

2. **To point:** Pick the next point along the leader line. Continue to pick points as you would in drawing a line. When you are finished, press ↵.

3. **Dimension text <default dimension>:** Press ↵ to accept the default or enter new dimension text.

● **NOTES**   The distance between the Leader start point and the next point must be at least twice the length of the arrow, or an arrow will not be placed.

If the last line segment of the leader is not horizontal, a horizontal line segment is added, as illustrated in Figure 17.

You can append text to the default dimension value. The default value is usually the last dimension entered. See Appending Dimension Text.

See Also   Dimension Variables: Dimasz, Dimscale

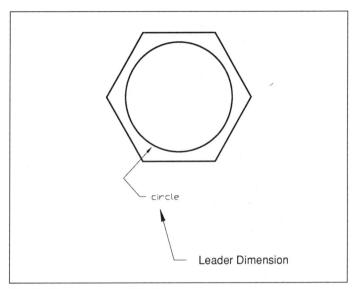

Figure 17: A segmented leader

LIMITS

- **VERSIONS**   All versions

- **PURPOSE**   Determines the drawing boundaries. If you use a grid, it will appear only within the limits.

In version 11, Limits sets the limits for Paperspace and Modelspace independently.

To Establish Drawing Boundaries

- From the keyboard: **Limit** ↵

- From the screen menu: **Settings-Limit**

- From the pull-down menu: **Utility-Limits** (11)

Then complete the following step:

ON/OFF/<lower left corner> <0.0000,0.0000>: Enter the coordinate for the lower-left corner or select the On/Off option.

● OPTIONS

ON   Turns on the limit-checking function. This keeps your drawing activity within the drawing limits.

OFF   Turns off the limit-checking function. This allows you to draw objects without respect to the drawing limits.

<lower left corner >   Allows you to set the drawing limits by entering the lower-left and upper-right corners of the desired limits.

● **NOTES**   Turn on the limit-checking feature and then perform a Zoom/All operation to make the virtual screen conform to the limits of the drawing.

The Setup option on the root menu or, in version 11, the Mvsetup option on the Bonus menu, will set the limits of your drawing automatically, according to the sheet size and drawing scale you select.

For version 11, the limits for Paperspace must be set independently of the Modelspace limits.

See Also   Limcheck, Limmax, Limmin, Mspace, Mview, Pspace, Regen, Viewres, Zoom

LINE

● **VERSIONS**   All versions

● **PURPOSE**   Draws simple lines, either a single line or a series of lines end-to-end.

To Draw a Line

- From the keyboard: **Line**⏎
- From the screen menu: **Draw-Line**
- From the pull-down menu: **Draw-Line**

Then follow these steps:

1. **From point:** Select a point to begin the line.
2. **To point:** Select the line end point.
3. **To point:** Continue to select points to draw consecutive lines or press ⏎ to exit the Line command.

● OPTIONS

C   Closes a series of lines

⏎   At the **from point** prompt, lets you continue a series of lines from a previously entered line, arc, point, or polyline. If the last object drawn is an arc, the line is drawn at a tangent from the end of the arc.

U   At the **From point** prompt, deletes the last line segment.

● **NOTES**   You can convert lines to polylines using the Pedit command.

See Also   Pedit, Pline

LINETYPE

● **VERSIONS**   2.0 and later

● **PURPOSE**   Linetype enables you to control the type of line you can draw. The default line type is continuous, but you can choose

from several other types, such as a dotted or dashed line or a combination of the two (see Figure 18). Several predefined line types are
stored in a file called Acad.LIN. You can list these line types by entering a question mark at the **Linetype** prompt.

To Change the Line Type

- From the keyboard: **Linetype** ⏎

- From the screen menu: **Settings-Linetype**

Then complete the following step:

   ?/Create/Load/Set: Enter the option name.

● OPTIONS

?   Lists available line types in a specified external line type file.
Version 11 displays the Files dialog box, which allows you to select
from a list.

Create   Creates a new line type. Version 11 displays the Files
dialog box, which allows you to select a line type file in which to
place your new line type definition.

Load   Loads a line type from a specified line type file. In version
11, the Load LType option on the Utility pull-down menu automatically issues this option. You select the file for the line type definition from the files dialog box.

Set   Sets the current default line type.

● NOTES   The Create option first prompts you for a line type

name. This name can be any alphanumeric string of eight characters
or less. You are then prompted for the name of the file in which to
store your line type. Next, you enter a description of the line type.
Finally, you enter the line type pattern on the next line, where you
will see an A followed by a comma and the cursor. Enter a string of
numeric values separated by commas. The positive values represent
the "drawn" portion of the line; the negative values represent the
"pen-up," or blank, portion of the line. These values should represent the lengths of lines as they will be plotted.

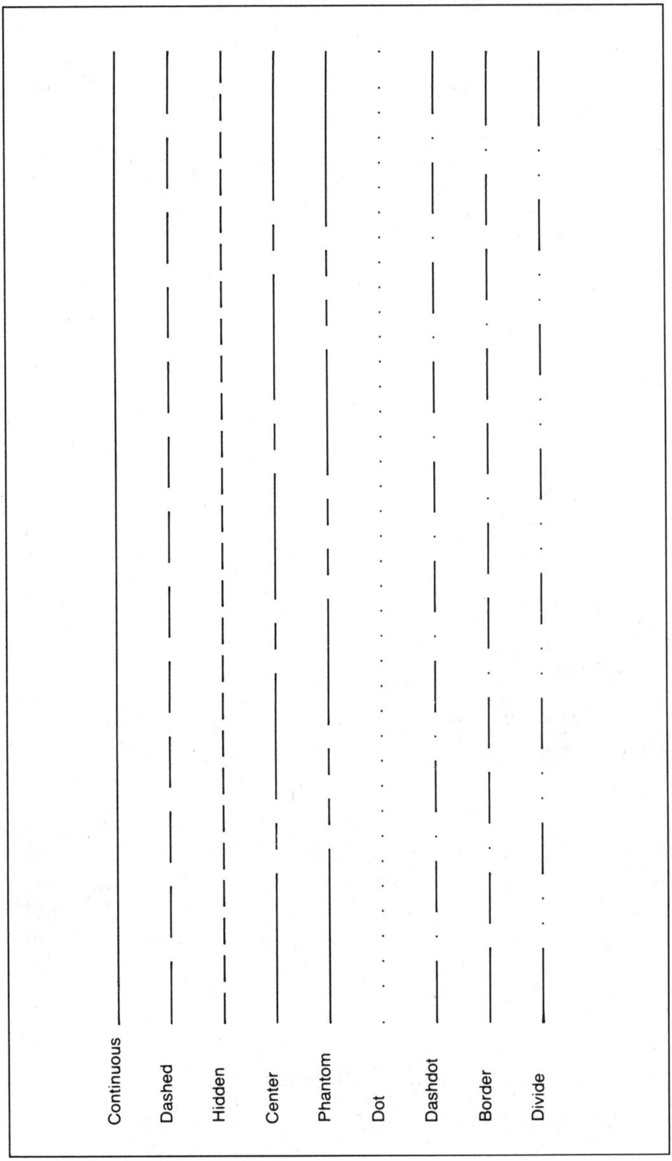

Figure 18: The standard AutoCAD line types

You can assign line types to layers or to individual objects. Use the Ltscale command to make the scale of the line types correspond with the scale of your drawing.

A line type may appear continuous even though it is a noncontinuous type. Several things can affect the appearance of line types. For example, if the drawing scale is not 1:1, the Ltscale must be set to correspond with your drawing scale. If the drawing scale is ¼" equals 1', the Ltscale must be set to 48. A low Viewres value can also affect appearance, making line types appear continuous on-screen even though they plot as a noncontinuous line type.

To assign line types using the Ddemodes and Ddlmodes command, first use the Linetype command to load the line type you want. In version 11, you can load line types using the Load LTypes option on the Utility pull-down menu.

See Also Celtype, Ddemodes, Ddlmodes, Layer, Ltscale, Viewres

LIST

● **VERSIONS** All versions

● **PURPOSE** Displays most of the properties of an object, including coordinate location, color, layer, and line type. Informs you if the object is a block or text. If the object is text, List gives its height, style, and width factor. If the object is a block, List gives its X, Y, and Z scale and insertion point. Attribute tags, defaults, and current values are also listed. If the object is a polyline, the coordinate values for all its vertices are listed.

To List Properties of an Object

•   From the keyboard: **List** ↵

•   From the screen menu: **Inquiry-List**

- From the pull-down menu: **Utility-List** (11)

Then complete the following step:

Select objects: Pick the objects whose properties you wish to see.

See Also   Dblist

LLOAD (AUTOLISP)

- **VERSIONS**   11

- **PURPOSE**   Eases loading of AutoLISP and ADS (AutoCAD Development Systems) utilities and applications.

Sequence of Steps

- From the keyboard: **(load "<drive>:/<path>/Lload")**↵ **LL**↵

- From the screen menu: **Bonus-next-Lload**

Then complete the following step:

If this is the first time this utility is used, you receive the prompt:
Build a new default file? <Y>:

A numbered list of AutoLISP utilities and ADS applications appears followed by the prompt:
Add/Remove an entry/<number to load>:

Enter the number corresponding to the item you want to load, or enter an option.

- **OPTIONS**

Add   Adds the name of an existing utility to the current list.

Remove an entry   Deletes an item from the list.

● **NOTES**   The first time you use this utility, you won't see any list. You must build your own list using the Add option. The utilities you want to add must be in the DOS path or in the AutoCAD directory that contains support files.

Once Lload is loaded, enter **LL** to load AutoLISP utilities and **XL** to load ADS utilities. Enter **UL** to unload ADS utilities. You can't unload AutoLISP utilities unless you exit a drawing file.

See Also   AutoLISP

LOAD

● **VERSIONS**   All versions

● **PURPOSE**   Loads a shape definition file. Like text and blocks, shapes are single objects made up of lines and arcs.

Sequence of Steps

•   From the keyboard: **Load** ↵

Then complete the following step:

In version 11, the Files dialog box appears. Earlier versions will display the following prompt:

Name of shape file to load (or ?):

Enter the name of the shape file, excluding the .shx file extension.

● **NOTES**   You can define shapes using the Shape code. Consult your *AutoCAD Reference Manual* for details. You can use shape definitions in place of blocks for frequently used symbols. They draw more quickly and use less file space.

See Also   Shape

LTSCALE

- **VERSIONS**   2.0 and later

- **PURPOSE**   Controls the scale of line types. Normally, line type definitions are created for a scale of 1:1. For larger scale drawings, 1:20 for example, set Ltscale so that line types fit the drawing scale. Ltscale globally adjusts all line type definitions to the value you give to Ltscale.

To Set the Scale of Linetypes

- From the keyboard: **Ltscale** ↲

Then complete the following step:

New scale factor <current default>: <scale factor>

If Regenauto is on, the drawing will regenerate once you enter a new scale factor.

- **NOTES**   Ltscale forces a drawing regeneration when Regenauto is on. If Regenauto is turned off, you won't see the effects of Ltscale until you issue Regen.

See Also   Linetype

MEASURE

• **VERSIONS**   2.5 and later

• **PURPOSE**   Marks an object into equal divisions of a specified length. Measurement begins at the end of the object closest to the pick point.

Sequence of Steps

- From the keyboard: **Measure⏎**

- From the screen menu: **Edit-next-Measure**

- From the pull-down menu: **Modify-Measure**

Then follow these steps:

1. **Select object to measure:** Pick a single object.

2. **<Segment length>/Block:** Enter the length of the segments to mark or the name of the block to use for marking.

• **OPTIONS**

Block   Establishes an existing, user-defined block as a marking device. You are prompted for a block name and asked if you want to align the block with the object.

• **NOTES**   By default, Measure uses a point as a marker. Often, a point is difficult to see when placed over a line or arc. Set the Pdmode and Pdsize system variables to change the appearance of the points, or select the Block option and use a block in place of the point.

The Block option is useful if you need to draw a series of objects a specified distance apart along a curved path.

See Also   Block, Divide, Point

MEMORY ALLOCATION (DOS)

- **VERSIONS**   9, 10, 11, AutoCAD for DOS (not 386 version)

- **PURPOSE**   Adjusts the amount of RAM DOS allocates to AutoCAD for work space, the amount of memory for AutoLISP functions, and the amount and location of extended or expanded memory for temporary files.

Sequence of Steps

- From the DOS command line: **Set <Parameter>**↵

- **OPTIONS**

Adjusting Free RAM

The default value for RAM work space, or *free RAM,* is about **24K** (14K for versions 2.6 and 9). To adjust AutoCAD's free RAM, at the DOS prompt enter

set acadfreeram = ##

where ## is the number of K bytes. This value is lost when you turn your computer off or reset it, so you may want to add the Acadfreeram statement to your Autoexec.bat file. The maximum allowable value for Acadfreeram is 30 (20 to 24 for versions 2.6 and 9).

Adjusting Memory for AutoLISP

AutoCAD allocates two types of memory for AutoLISP: *heap* and *stack.* Very basically, heap stores functions and variables. This storage is also called *node space.* The stack holds arguments and partial results during the evaluation of expressions. The default values are 40K for Lispheap and 3K for Lispstack (or 5K each in versions 9 and earlier). In most cases, the heap is the limiting space.

If you get an insufficient node space message, exit from AutoCAD and, at the DOS prompt, enter the following:

>**set lispheap = #####**
>
>**set lispstack = ####**

where #### is the number of bytes. The total amount of heap and stack space cannot exceed 45K bytes. You may want to include these lines in your Autoexec.bat file.

Using Extended Memory for AutoLISP

Non-386 versions 10 and later of AutoCAD for DOS can use extended memory for AutoLISP. To use extended memory you must have version 2.0 or later of MS or PC DOS, 640K RAM for DOS, and 512K RAM of unused extended memory.

To use Extended AutoLISP, you must have the following files in your AutoCAD directory:

- Acadlx.OVL
- Extlisp.EXE
- Remlisp.EXE

Acadlx.OVL is a special overlay file. You must load Extlisp.EXE before you start AutoCAD. Remlisp.EXE allows you to unload Extlisp.EXE to free DOS memory.

In the AutoCAD directory, enter **Extlisp** at the DOS prompt and then start AutoCAD. Select option **5** from the Main menu to see a listing of your current AutoCAD configuration. Press ⏎. Enter 8 to open the Configure Operating Parameters menu. Enter **7** to select the AutoLISP features option. Enter **yes** when asked if you want AutoLISP enabled. Enter **yes** when asked if you want to use Extended AutoLISP. Exit to the Main menu. AutoCAD will now use extended memory for AutoLISP. From now on, you must load Extlisp.EXE before you start AutoCAD.

Adjusting Extended and Expanded Memory Use

If either extended or expanded memory is present in your computer, AutoCAD automatically uses it instead of disk space to speed up access to temporary files. Expanded memory is used first.

To set the amount of extended memory used for temporary files, enter the following at the DOS prompt before starting AutoCAD:

set acadxmem=<start_location,size>

The start location value can be anything between 1024K and 16384K. Type **K** following the **start** location and again following **size**. The size can be any number. The following example shows what to enter if you have 512K of extended memory, the upper 256K of which you wish to allocate to AutoCAD:

set acadxmem=1280k,256k

The start location in this example is 1280K, which equals 1024K + 256K. Omit the size value to allocate all of the remaining extended memory to AutoCAD. Omit the start location value if you want AutoCAD to select its own starting location. If you use only the size value, you still must precede the value with a comma. Enter **none** in place of the start location and size value to force AutoCAD to ignore extended memory.

To allocate memory for Extlisp, use Lispxmem instead of Acadxmem. You can also include the Acadxmem and Lispxmem settings in your Autoexec.bat file.

Setting Expanded Memory

To set expanded memory, enter the following at the DOS prompt before starting AutoCAD:

set acadlimem=<size>

The size can be specified in 16K increments or in exact amounts. For example, if you enter **20** for the size, AutoCAD will allocate itself $20 \times 16K$ or 320K of expanded memory. You can also enter **320K** to achieve the same result. Negative numbers cause AutoCAD to allocate itself all but the amount entered. To force AutoCAD to ignore expanded memory, enter **none** for the size value. You can include the Acadlimem setting in your Autoexec.bat file to avoid having to set it each time you open AutoCAD.

Allocating Memory for the DOS Environment

For versions 3.2 and 3.3 of DOS, you may run out of environment space for the preceding AutoCAD settings. If so, you usually get the following message:

Out of environment space.

You can increase the DOS environment size with the DOS Shell function. Place the following line in your config.sys file in the root directory of your hard disk drive:

shell=c:\command.com /e:512 /p

The DOS environment is usually given 128 bytes. The preceding example increases that size to 512 bytes. This is usually enough for AutoCAD and other settings.

If you do not have a config.sys file, use DOS's COPY CON command or the Edlin line editor and create an ASCII file containing the following lines:

SHELL=C:\ COMMAND.COM /E:512 /P
FILES=20
BUFFERS=32

The files=20 statement tells DOS to allow up to 20 open files at once. AutoCAD opens many temporary files in the course of its operation. Setting Files to 20 will improve AutoCAD's performance. The Buffers=32 statement tells DOS to store in RAM the information most recently read from the hard disk. Buffers improves overall disk access speed.

See Also   Cfig386.EXE

MENU

● **VERSIONS**   All versions

● **PURPOSE**   Loads a custom menu file. Once you have loaded
a menu into a drawing, that drawing file will include the menu file
name. The next time you open the drawing file, AutoCAD will also
attempt to load the last menu used with the file.

To Load a Custom Menu

- From the keyboard: **Menu↵**

- From the screen menu: **Utility-Menu**

Then complete the following step:

Version 11 displays the files dialog box. Earlier versions display the following prompt:
Menu file name or . for none <acad>: Enter the menu file
name.

See Also   Menuname

MFACE (AUTOLISP)

● **VERSIONS**   11

● **PURPOSE**   Mface is an alternative to the Pface command. It
simplifies the construction of a polyface mesh by automatically
making adjacent Pface edges invisible.

Sequence of Steps

- From the keyboard: **(load "<drive>:/<path>/mface")↵
  Mface↵**

- From the screen menu: **Bonus-next-Mface**

Then complete the following step:

Layer/Color/<Select vertex>: Pick points to define the vertices of the Pface mesh or enter an option. When you begin to pick points, the following prompt appears:

Select vertex:

Pick points to indicate the vertices of the polyface mesh. To change a color or layer, press ⏎. The **Layer/Color** prompt returns.

● OPTIONS

Layer   Sets layer on which to draw a Pface edge.

Color   Sets the color of a Pface edge.

● **Notes**   From the keyboard, you have to load Mface only once per editing session. You can then use Mface at any time. It is not necessary to load Mface if you are using the menu.

See Also   Pface

MINSERT

● **VERSIONS**   2.5 and later

● **PURPOSE**   Simultaneously inserts a block and creates a rectangular array of that block. You can rotate the array by specifying an angle other than 0 at the **Rotation angle** prompt.

Sequence of Steps

•   From the keyboard: **Minsert** ⏎

•   From the screen menu: **Blocks-Minsert**

Then follow these steps:

The prompts for Minsert are the same as for Insert, except for the following:

1. **Rotation Angle <0>:** Enter the array angle.
2. **Number of rows (---) <1>:** Enter the number of rows in the block array.
3. **Number of columns (| | |) <1>:** Enter the number of columns in the block array.

If the number of rows or columns is greater than one, one of the following prompts appears:

4. **Unit cell or distance between rows (---):** Enter a distance or select the distance using the cursor.
5. **Distance between columns (| | |):** Enter the distance or select the distance using the cursor.

If both rows and columns are greater than one, you will get both prompts. A row and column array of the block will appear at the specified angle.

● **NOTES**   The entire array acts like one block. You cannot explode a block or use the asterisk option (see Insert) on a block inserted with Minsert.

See Also   Array, Insert

MIRROR

● **VERSIONS**   2.5 and later

● **PURPOSE**   Makes a mirror-image copy of an object or a group of objects.

Sequence of Steps

- From the keyboard: **Mirror.⏎**
- From the screen menu: **Edit-next-Mirror**
- From the pull-down menu: **Modify-Mirror**

Then follow these steps:

1. **Select objects:** Pick the objects to be mirrored.

2. **First point of mirror line:** Pick one end of the mirror axis.

3. **Second point:** Pick the other end of the mirror axis.

4. **Delete old objects? <N>** Enter **Y** to delete the originally selected objects or **N** to keep them.

● **NOTES**   Normally, text and attributes are mirrored. To prevent this, set the Mirrtext system variable to 0.

Mirroring occurs in a plane parallel to the current UCS.

See Also   Mirrtext

MOVE

● **VERSIONS**   All versions

● **PURPOSE**   Moves a single object or a set of objects.

Sequence of Steps

- From the keyboard: **Move.⏎**
- From the screen menu: **Edit-next-Move**
- From the pull-down menu: **Edit-Move** (9), **Modify-Move** (10, 11)

Then follow these steps:

1. **Select objects:** Select the objects to be moved.

2. **Base point or displacement:** Pick the reference or "base" point for the move.

3. **Second point of displacement:** Pick the move distance and direction in relation to the base point or enter the displacement value.

● **NOTES**   AutoCAD assumes you want to move objects within the current UCS. However, you can move objects in three-dimensional space by entering X,Y,Z coordinates or using the Osnap overrides to pick objects in three-dimensional space.

If you press ↵ at the **Second point** prompt without entering a point value, the objects selected may be moved to a position completely off your drawing area. Use the U or Undo command to recover.

MSLIDE

● **VERSIONS**   All versions

● **PURPOSE**   Mslide saves the current view in a Slide file. (Slide files have .SLD extensions).

To Save in an SLD File

• From the keyboard: **Mslide**↵

• From the screen menu: **Utility-Slides-Mslide**

Then complete the following step:

Version 11 displays a Files dialog box. Earlier versions display the following prompt:

File name <current file name>: Enter desired file name, excluding extension.

See Also Vslide

MSPACE

● **VERSIONS** 11

● **PURPOSE** Mspace lets you move from Paperspace to Modelspace.

Sequence of Steps

• From the keyboard: **Mspace⏎**

• From the screen menu: **Mview-Mspace**

• From the pull-down menu: **Display-Mview-Mspace**

AutoCAD switches to Modelspace. If the Tilemode system variable is not set to 0, you will receive the message:

There are no active Modelspace Viewports.

See Also Mview, Pspace, Tilemode

MULTIPLE

● **VERSIONS** 2.5 and later

• **PURPOSE**   Multiple lets you enact multiple repeats of a command.

To Repeat a Command

• From the keyboard: **Multiple <command to repeat>**⏎

MVIEW

• **VERSIONS**   11

• **PURPOSE**   Creates Paperspace viewport entities and controls the visibility of viewports in Paperspace. This command only works in Paperspace.

To Create a Paperspace Viewport

• From the keyboard: **Mview**⏎

• From the screen menu: **Mview**

• From the pull-down menu: **Display-Mview**

Then complete the following step:

ON/OFF/Hideplot/Fit/2/3/4/Restore/<First point>: Pick a point indicating one corner of the new Paperspace viewport or enter an option.

If you pick a point, you are prompted for the opposite corner. Mview then creates the viewport.

• **OPTIONS**

ON/OFF   Turns the display of Modelspace on or off within the chosen viewport. When a viewport's Modelspace display is turned off, it no longer regenerates when it is moved or re-sized. This is helpful when you are re-arranging a set of viewports.

Hideplot   Controls hidden line removal for individual viewports at plot time. When you select this option, the select objects prompt appears. Pick the viewport you wish to have plotted with hidden lines removed.

Fit   Creates a single viewport that fills the screen.

2/3/4   Lets you create 2, 3, or 4 viewports simultaneously. Once you enter one of these options, the prompt **Fit/<first point>** appears. Pick points to indicate the location of the viewports, or select the Fit option to force the viewports to fit in the display area. If you choose Fit, you are further prompted for the orientation of the viewports.

Restore   Translates viewport configurations created using the Vport command (Modelspace Viewports) into Paperspace viewport entities. You are prompted to enter the name of a viewport configuration.

● **NOTES**   The Tilemode system variable must be set to 0 to use Mview. If you are in Modelspace when you issue Mview, you receive the message:

Switching to Paperspace.

Grid and Snap modes as well as layer visibility can be set individually within each Paperspace viewport.

Viewports, like most other entities, can be moved, copied, stretched, or erased. You can hide viewport borders by changing their layer assignments, then turning off their layers. You can also align positions of objects in one viewport with those of another using the Mvsetup utility. Viewport scale can be set using the **xp** option under the Zoom command.

See Also   Mspace, Mvsetup, Pspace, Tilemode, Vplayer, Vports, Zoom/xp

MVSETUP (AUTOLISP)

● **VERSIONS**   11

● **PURPOSE**   Sets up the Paperspace of a drawing including viewports, drawing scale, and sheet title block. It also takes over the functions of the Setup utility found on the main menu of versions 9 and 10.

To Set up a Paperspace

●   From the keyboard: **(load "<drive>:/<path>/Mvsetup")**⤶ **Mvs**⤶

●   From the screen menu: **Bonus-next-Mvsetup**

Then complete the following step:

On a new drawing with Tilemode set to 1, the following prompt appears:

Paperspace/Modelspace is disabled. The old setup will be invoked unless it is enabled. Enable Paper/Modelspace?<Y>:

Enter **No** to use the setup method in versions 9 and 10 of AutoCAD (see Setup). If you press ⤶ to accept the default **Y**, set the Tilemode system variable to 0, and bring up the following prompt:

Align viewports/Create viewports/Scale viewports /Title block/Undo:

● **OPTIONS**

Align viewports   Aligns locations in one viewport with locations in another viewport. You receive the prompt **Angled/Horizontal/Vertical alignment/Rotate view/Undo:**.

Angled   Aligns locations by indicating an angle and distance. You are prompted to pick a base point to which others can be aligned. Next, you are prompted to pick a point in another viewport that you want aligned with the base point. You are then prompted for a distance and angle.

Horizontal/Vertical alignment   Aligns views either horizontally or vertically. You are prompted for a base point (the point to be aligned to) and the point to be aligned with the base point.

Rotate view   Rotates a view in a viewport. You are prompted for a viewport and base point, and the angle of rotation.

Create viewports   Creates new viewports. You receive the prompt **Delete objects/Undo/<Create viewports>:**.

Delete objects   Deletes existing viewport entities. **<Create viewports>** displays a list of options for creating viewports:

0: None
1: Single
2: Std. Engineering
3: Array of Viewports
Add/Delete/Redisplay/<Number of entry to load>:

0 (None) creates no viewports. 1 (Single) creates a single viewport for which you specify the area. 2 (Std. Engineering) creates four viewports set up in quadrants. You can set up these views for top, front, right side, and isometric. 3 (Array of Viewports) creates a matrix of viewports by specifying the number of viewports in the X- and Y-axes. The Add/Delete option on the prompt adds or deletes options from the list. Add provides a title block for the list. Redisplay lets you view the list again.

Scale viewports   Sets the scale between Paperspace and the viewport. For example, if your drawing in Modelspace is ¼" = 1' scale, and your title block in Paperspace is at a scale of 1" = 1", you will want the scale factor of your viewport to be 48. When you select this option the prompt **Select the viewports to scale:** appears. Once you've made a selection, the prompt **Set zoom scale factors for viewports. Interactively/<Uniform>:** appears. The Interactively option sets the scale of each selected viewport individually. You are prompted for the number of Paperspace units, then the number of corresponding Modelspace units. In the ¼" scale example, you would enter **1** for the Paperspace units and 48 for the Modelspace units. The <Uniform> option sets all viewports to the same scale.

Title block   Produces the prompt **Delete objects/Origin/ Undo/<Insert title block>:**. Delete objects removes selected items from Paperspace. Origin sets a new origin point for Paperspace. <Insert title block> displays the following:

Available paper/output sizes:

0: None
1: ANSI-V Size
2: ANSI-A Size
3: ANSI-B Size
4: ANSI-C Size
5: ANSI-D Size
6: ANSI-E Size
7: Arch/Engineering (24 × 36)
Add/Delete/Redisplay/<Number of entry to load>:

Enter the number corresponding to the title block you want to use. Add and Delete let you add or delete a title block to the list. Add prompts you for the name you wish to have appear on the list and the name of the file to be used as the title block. Redisplay lets you view the list again.

Undo   Undoes an option without leaving the Mvsetup utility.

● **NOTES**   When adding a title block to the list in the title block option, you must already have a title block drawing ready and in the current DOS path.

The Xp option under the Zoom command can also be used to set the scale of a viewport.

From the keyboard, you have to reload Mvsetup only once per editing session. You can then use Mvsetup at any time. It is not necessary to load Mvsetup if you are using the menu.

See Also   Mspace, Mview, Pspace, Setup, Tilemode, Zoom

NEWTEXT (DIM)

● **VERSIONS**   2.6 and later

● **PURPOSE**   Edits associative dimension text in several dimensions at once.

Before Dimensioning

You must have issued the Dim or Dim1 command to use any dimensioning subcommand.

Sequence of Steps

- From the keyboard: **Newtext** ↵

- From the screen menu: **Dim-next-Newtext**

Then follow these steps:

1. **Enter new dimension text:** Enter text. You can also use the <> signs to append text to the current text.

2. **Select objects:** Pick the dimensions to be edited.

● **NOTES**   At **Select objects:** select one or several dimensions. All associative dimensions selected will be changed to the new text.

OBLIQUE (DIM)

● **VERSIONS**   11

● **PURPOSE**   Skews existing dimension extension lines to an angle of other than 90 degrees to the dimension line.

Before Dimensioning

You must have issued the Dim or Dim1 command to use any dimensioning subcommand.

To Skew Extension Lines

- From the keyboard: **Oblique** ⏎

- From the screen menu: **Dim-Oblique**

Then follow these steps:

1. **Select objects:** Pick the dimensions to be edited.

2. **Enter obliquing angle (RETURN for none):** Enter the desired angle for extension lines.

● **NOTES**   If the dimension being edited has a dimension style setting, then this setting is maintained. If no style is associated with the dimension, the current dimension variable settings are used to update the obliqued dimension.

See Also   Dimstyle

OFFSET

● **VERSIONS**   2.5 and later

● **PURPOSE**   Offset creates an object parallel to and at a specified distance from its original.

Sequence of Steps

- From the keyboard: **Offset** ⏎

- From the screen menu: **Edit-next-Offset**

- From the pull-down menu: **Modify-Offset** (10, 11)

Then follow these steps:

1. **Offset distance or Through <default distance>:** Enter a
   distance value to specify a constant distance or **Through**
   to specify an offset distance after each object selection is
   made.

2. **Select object to offset:** Pick one object.

3. **Side to offset:** Pick the side on which you want the offset
   to appear.

● OPTIONS

Distance   If you enter a value at the **Distance** prompt, all the offsets performed in the current command will be at that distance.
Enter **T** at this prompt to specify a different offset distance for each
object selected.

Through   Identifies a point through which the offset object will
pass after you have selected the object to offset. You will be
prompted for a distance after each object is selected.

● NOTES   Very complex polylines may offset incorrectly or not
at all. This usually means there is insufficient memory to process the
offset.

You can only perform offsets on objects that lie in a plane parallel to
the current UCS. Also, if you are not viewing the current UCS in
plan, you may get an erroneous result.

See Also   Copy

OOPS

● VERSIONS   2.0 and later

● **PURPOSE**   Oops restores objects that have been accidentally removed from a drawing.

To Restore an Object

- From the keyboard: **Oops** ↵

- From the pull-down menu: **Modify-Oops!**

See Also   U, Undo

ORDINATE (DIM)

● **VERSIONS**   11

● **PURPOSE**   Draws an ordinate dimension string based on a datum or origin point.

Sequence of Steps

Use the UCS command to create a UCS with its origin at the datum location. Then issue the Dim command to access the Ordinate dimension subcommand.

- From the keyboard: **Ordinate** ↵

- From the screen menu: **Dim-Ordinate**

Follow these steps:

1. **Select Feature:** Pick the location of the feature to be dimensioned.

2. **Leader endpoint (Xdatum/Ydatum):** Indicate the orientation of the dimension leader or enter X or Y to specify the axis along which the dimension is to be taken.

3. **Leader endpoint:** Pick the location of the leader endpoint.

• **NOTES**   If you pick a point at the first **Leader endpoint** prompt, then AutoCAD selects the dimension axis based on the angle defined by the points you pick during the **Select feature** and **Leader endpoint** prompts.

See Also   UCS

ORTHO

• **VERSIONS**   11

• **PURPOSE**   Ortho forces lines to be drawn in exactly vertical or horizontal directions.

Sequence of Steps

•   From the keyboard: **Ortho⤶ F8 Ctrl-O**

•   From the pull-down menu: **Settings-Ortho On/Off**

• **NOTES**   If you enter Ortho through the keyboard, you are prompted to turn Ortho on or off. Use the F8 function key or the Ctrl-O key combination to toggle between Ortho On and Ortho Off.

To force lines to angles other than 90 degrees, rotate the cursor using the Snapang system variable or by setting the Rotate option under the Snap command.

See Also   Ddrmodes, Snap, Snapang

OSNAP

• **VERSIONS**   2.0 and later

• **PURPOSE**   Sets the current default Object Snap mode, allowing you to pick specific geometric points on an object. You can have
several Object Snap modes active at once if you separate their names
by commas. For example, to be able to select endpoints and midpoints automatically, enter **END,MID** at the **Osnap** prompt.
AutoCAD knows to select the correct point (MID, END, etc.),
depending on which point is closer to the target box.

To Pick Specific Geometric Points

• From the keyboard: **Osnap.**⏎

• From the screen menu: **Settings-next-Osnap**

• From the pull-down menu: **Tools-Osnap** (9, 10), **Assist-
Osnap** (11)

Then complete the following step:

Object snap modes: Enter the desired default Object snap
mode(s).

• **OPTIONS**

CENter   Picks the center of circles and arcs.

ENDpoint   Picks the end point of objects.

INSert   Picks the insertion point of blocks and text.

INTersect   Picks the intersection of objects.

MIDpoint   Picks the midpoint of lines and arcs.

NEArest   Picks the point on an object nearest to the cursor.

NODe   Picks a point object.

PERpend   Picks the point on an object perpendicular to the last
point.

QUAdrant   Picks a cardinal point on an arc or circle.

Quick   Shortens the time it takes AutoCAD to find an object snap
point. Quick does not work in conjunction with INTersect.

Tangent   Picks a tangent point on a circle or arc.

NONE   Disables the current default Object snap mode.

● **NOTES**   You can use the Osnap overrides whenever you are prompted to select a point or object. Enter the first three letters of the name of the override or pick the override from the Assist pull-down menu, Tools pull-down menu, or Asterisks side menu. Unlike the Osnap mode settings, the overrides are active only at the time they are issued.

See Also   Aperture

OVERRIDE (DIM)

● **VERSIONS**   11

● **PURPOSE**   Changes an individual associative dimension's properties, such as its arrow style, colors, scale, text orientation, etc. Also modifies a dimension style by allowing you to alter the dimension variable settings associated with a dimension or dimension style.

Before Dimensioning

You must have issued the Dim or Dim1 command to use any dimensioning subcommand.

To Change
an Associative Dimension's Properties

● From the keyboard: **Override** ↵

● From the screen menu: **Dim-Override**

Then follow these steps:

1. **Dimension variable to override:** Enter the dimension variable name.

2. **Current value <(variables value)> New value:** Enter the new value.

3. **Dimension variable to override:** Enter another dimension variable name or ↵ to continue.

4. **Select objects:** Select the dimension(s) to be changed.

If the selected dimension is associated with a dimension style, the following prompt appears:

5. **Modify dimension style "style name"? <N>:** Enter Y for yes or ↵.

If you enter Y, the style indicated by the prompt will be updated with the new setting(s). If you enter N or ↵, only the selected associative dimension(s) will change.

See Also   Dimstyle, Restore

PAN

● **VERSIONS**   All versions. Transparent capability added in version 2.5.

● **PURPOSE**   Shifts the display to reveal parts of a drawing that are offscreen. When picked from the menu system or when keyed in with an apostrophe preceding the name, Pan can be used in the middle of another command.

To See Offscreen Drawing Areas

• From the keyboard: **Pan**↵

- From the screen menu: **Display-Pan**

- From the pull-down menu: **Display-Pan**

Then follow these steps:

1. **Displacement:** Pick the first point of view displacement.

2. **Second point:** Pick the distance and direction of displacement.

● **NOTES** You cannot use Pan while viewing a drawing in perspective. Use the Dview command's Pan option instead.

See Also Dview/Pan, View, Zoom

PEDIT

● **VERSIONS** 2.1 and later

● **PURPOSE** Edits two-dimensional or three-dimensional polylines and three-dimensional meshes, changes the location of individual vertices in a polyline or mesh, and converts a non-polyline object into a polyline. The editing options available depend on the type of object you select. See the following sections for information about individual Pedit operations.

To Edit 3D Polylines and Meshes

- From the keyboard: **Pedit**↵

- From the screen menu: **Edit-next-Pedit**

- From the pull-down menu: **Edit-Polyedit** (9), **Modify-Edit-Polylines**, **Modify-Polyedit**

Then complete the following step:

1. **Select polyline:** Select the polyline or three-dimensional mesh.

PEDIT FOR 2D AND 3D POLYLINES

● **PURPOSE**   Modifies the shape of 2D and 3D polylines. If the object you select is not a polyline, you are asked whether you want to turn it into one.

To Edit Polylines

• If the object selected is a two-dimensional polyline, the following prompt appears:

   Close/Join/Width/Edit vertex/Fit curve/Spline curve/Decurve/Undo/eXit <X>: <option>

• If the object is a three-dimensional polyline, the following prompt appears:

   Close/Edit vertex/Spline curve/Decurve/Undo/eXit <X>: <option>

• If the object is a standard line or arc, the following prompt appears:

   **Entity selected is not a polyline
   Do you want it to turn into one: <Y>:**

   Enter **Y** or **N**.

● **OPTIONS**

Close   Joins the end points of a polyline. If the selected polyline is already closed, this option is replaced by Open in the prompt.

Open   Deletes the last line segment in a closed polyline.

Join   Joins polylines, lines, and arcs. The objects to be joined must meet exactly end-to-end.

Width   Sets the width of the entire polyline.

Edit vertex   Performs various edits on polyline vertices. See Pedit/Edit vertex in this chapter.

Fit curve   Changes a polyline made up of straight line segments into a smooth curve.

Spline curve   Changes a polyline made up of straight line segments into a smooth spline curve.

Decurve   Changes a smoothed polyline into one made up of straight line segments.

Undo   Rescinds the last Pedit function issued.

eXit   Exits the Pedit command.

● **NOTES**   The Spline curve option adjusts the "pull" of the vertex points on the curve by changing the Spline system variable. The default for Splinetype is 6. With Splinetype set to 5, the pull is greater. See Setvar for more details.

You can view both the curve and the defining vertex points of a Spline curve by setting the Splframe system variable to 1.

The Splinesegs system variable determines the number of line segments used to draw the curve. A higher value generates more line segments for a smoother curve, but also a larger drawing file.

See Also   Pedit/3D mesh, Pedit/Edit Vertex, Pline, Setvar/Splframe, Setvar/Splinesegs, Setvar/Splinetype

PEDIT/EDIT VERTEX

● **VERSIONS**   2.1 and later

● **PURPOSE**   Relocates, removes, or moves vertices in a polyline. Modifies a polyline's width at a particular vertex and alters the tangent direction of a curved polyline through a vertex.

To Edit a Polyline Vertex

Once you've issued the Pedit command and selected a polyline, you get the following prompt:

1. **Close/Join/Width/Edit vertex/Fit curve/Decurve/ Undo/eXit <X>:** Enter **E**. An X appears on the selected polyline indicating the vertex currently editable.

2. **Next/Previous/Break/Insert/Move/Regen/Straighten/ Tangent/Width/eXit <N>:** Enter the capitalized letter of the function to be used.

● **OPTIONS**

Next   Moves the X marker to the next vertex.

Previous   Moves the X marker to the previous vertex.

Break   Breaks polyline from the marked vertex. Once you select Break, you can move the marker to another vertex to select the other end of the break. When this function is entered, the prompt changes to

Next/Previous/Go/eXit <N>:

allowing you to move in either direction along the polyline. Once the X marker is in position, enter **G** to initiate the break.

Insert   Inserts a new vertex. A rubber-banding line stretches from the vertex being edited to the cursor. Enter points either using the cursor or by keying in coordinates.

Move   Allows relocation of a vertex. A rubber-banding line stretches from the vertex being edited to the cursor. You can specify points by using either the cursor or by keying in coordinates.

Regen   Regenerates a polyline. This may be required to see effects of some edits.

Straighten   Straightens a polyline between two vertices. When you enter this function, the prompt changes to

Next/Previous/Go/eXit <N>:

This allows you to move in either direction along the polyline. Once the X marker (see Notes) is in position, type **G** to straighten the polyline.

Tangent   Modifies the tangent direction of a vertex. A rubber-banding line stretches from the vertex to the cursor, indicating the new tangent direction. Indicate the new tangent angle by picking the direction using the cursor or by keying in an angle value. Tangent only affects curve-fitted or spline polylines.

Width   Varies the width of a polyline segment. When you have entered this function, the prompt changes to

Enter starting width <current default width>:

This allows you to enter a new width for the currently marked vertex. When you have entered a value, the prompt changes to:

Enter ending width <last value entered>:

This allows you to enter a width for the next vertex.

eXit   Exits from vertex editing.

● **NOTES**   When you invoke the Edit Vertex option, an X appears on the polyline, indicating that the vertex is being edited. Press ↵ to move the X to the next vertex. Type **P** to reverse the direction of the X. When inserting a new vertex or using the width function, pay special attention to the direction the X moves when you select the Next function. This is the direction along the polyline in which the new vertex or the new ending width will be inserted.

If you select a three-dimensional polyline, all the edit options except Tangent and Width are available. Also, point input accepts three-dimensional points.

PEDIT FOR 3D MESHES

● **VERSIONS**   10, 11

● **PURPOSE**   Smoothes a three-dimensional mesh or moves vertex points in the mesh.

To Edit a 3D Mesh

Once you have issued the Pedit command and selected a mesh, you get the prompt:

**Edit vertex/Smooth surface/Desmooth/Mclose/
Nclose/Undo/eXit <X>: <option>**

● **OPTIONS**

Edit vertex   Relocates vertices of a selected three-dimensional mesh. When you select this option, you get the prompt:

**Vertex (m,n)
Next/Previous/Left/Right/Up/Down/Move/REgen/eXit
<N>: <option>**

An X appears on the first vertex of the mesh, marking the vertex to be moved.

Next   Rapidly moves the Edit vertex marker to the next vertex.

Previous   Rapidly moves the Edit vertex marker to the previous vertex.

Left   Moves the Edit vertex marker along the N direction of the mesh.

Right   Moves the Edit vertex marker along the N direction of the mesh opposite to the Left option.

Up   Moves the Edit vertex marker along the M direction of the mesh.

Down   Moves the Edit vertex marker along the M direction of the mesh opposite to the Up direction.

Move   Moves the location of the currently marked vertex.

REgen   Redisplays the mesh after a vertex has been moved.

Smooth surface   Generates a B-spline or Bezier surface based on the mesh's vertex points. The type of surface generated depends on the Surftype system variable.

Desmooth   Returns a smoothed surface back to regular mesh.

Mclose   Closes a mesh in the M direction.

Nclose   Closes a mesh in the N direction.

Undo   Rescinds the last Pedit option issued.

eXit   Exits the Edit vertex option or the Pedit command.

● **NOTES**   You can use several system variables (see Setvar) to modify a three-dimensional mesh. To determine the type of smooth surface generated, use the Surftype variable with the Smooth option. A value of 5 gives you a quadratic B-spline surface; 6, a cubic B-spline surface; 8, a Bezier surface. The default value for Surftype is 6.

The Surfu and Surfv system variables control the accuracy of the generated surface. Surfu controls the surface density in the M direction of the mesh while Surfv controls density in the N direction. The default value for these variables is 6.

The Splframe system variable determines whether the control mesh of a smoothed mesh is displayed. If it is set to 0, only the smoothed mesh is displayed. If set to 1, only the defining mesh is displayed.

See Also   Splframe, Surftype, Surfu, Surfv

PFACE

● **VERSIONS**   11

● **PURPOSE**   Draws a polygon mesh by first defining the vertices of the mesh then assigning 3Dfaces to the vertex locations.

To Draw a Polygon Mesh

- From the keyboard: **Pface** ↵

- From the screen menu: **Draw-next-3D Surfs-Pface**

Then follow these steps:

1. **Vertex 1:** Pick a point for the first vertex used in defining the mesh. The vertex prompt repeats after each point is selected. The vertex number increases by one each time you pick a point. Remember the location of each vertex; you will need to know the number for the next step. When you have finished selecting points, press ↵. You receive the following prompt:

2. **Face1, Vertex 1:** Enter the number of the vertex from step 1 that you want to correspond to the first vertex of the first face. When you enter a number, the same prompt appears with the vertex number increased by 1. You can define one face with as many of the points as you indicated in step 2. When you have defined the first face, press ↵. The prompt will change to the following:

3. **Face 2, Vertex 1:** Enter the number of the vertex that you want to correspond to the first vertex of the second face. When you are done, press ↵.

● OPTIONS

−n   Makes a face edge invisible when entered at the **Face *n*, Vertex *n*** prompt. You must use a negative value for each overlapping edge.

Layer   Specifies the layer for the face you are currently defining. Enter Layer at the **Face *n*, Vertex *n*** prompt.

Color   Specifies the color of the face you are currently defining Enter Color at the **Face *n*, Vertex *n*** prompt.

● **NOTES**   Pface was designed for programmers who need an entity type that can easily create three-dimensional surfaces with special properties. Pfaces cannot be edited using Pedit. However, you can use Array, Chprop, Copy, Erase, List, Mirror, Move, Rotate, Scale, Stretch, and explode on Pfaces.

See Also   Edgesurf, Mesh, Mface, Revsurf, Rulesurf, Tabsurf

PLAN

● **VERSIONS**   10, 11

● **PURPOSE**   Displays a user coordinate system in plan, that is, a view perpendicular to the UCS. This allows you to create and manipulate objects in 2D more easily. Plan affects only the active viewport. You can set the Ucsfollow system variable so that whenever you change to a different UCS, you get a plan view of it.

To View in Plan

- From the keyboard: **Plan**↵

- From the screen menu: **Display-Plan**

- From the pull-down menu: **Display-Plan View (UCS or World)**

Then complete the following step:

   <Current UCS>/Ucs/World: Enter the capitalized letter of the desired option or press ↵ for the current UCS.

● **OPTIONS**

↵   Gives you a plan view of the current UCS. This is the default option. It is automatically issued when you pick PlanView (UCS) from the Display pull-down menu.

U   Gives you a plan view of a previously saved UCS. You are prompted for the name of the UCS you wish to see in plan. Enter a question mark to get a list of saved UCSs.

W   Gives you a plan view of the world coordinate system. This option is automatically issued when you pick PlanView (world) from the Display pull-down menu.

See Also   UCS, Ucsfollow

PLINE

- **VERSIONS**   2.5 and later

- **PURPOSE**   Creates lines having properties such as thickness and curvature. Unlike standard lines, polylines can be grouped together to act as a single object. For example, a box you draw using a polyline will act as one object instead of four discrete lines.

To Create a Polyline

- From the keyboard: **Pline** ↵

- From the screen menu: **Draw-Pline**

- From the pull-down menu: **Draw-Polyline**

Then follow these steps:

1. **From point:** Pick the start point of the polyline.

2. **Arc/Close/Halfwidth/Length/Undo/Width/<Endpoint of line>:** Enter the desired option or pick the next point of the polyline.

- **OPTIONS**

Arc   Draws a polyline arc. You can enter either the second point, angle, center, direction, radius, or endpoint of the arc. See the Arc command for the use of the Arc options.

Close   Draws a line from the current polyline end point back to its beginning, forming a closed polyline.

Halfwidth   Specifies half the polyline width at the current point. You are first prompted for the starting half-width, which is half the width of the polyline at the last fixed point. Next, you are prompted for the ending half width—half the width of the polyline at the next point you pick.

Length   Draws a polyline in the same direction as the last line segment drawn. You are prompted for the line segment length. If an arc was drawn last, the direction will be tangent to the end direction of that arc.

Undo   Allows you to step backward along the current string of polyline or polyarc segments.

Width   Determines the whole width of the polyline. Subsequent polylines will be of this width unless you specify otherwise.

● **NOTES**   To give a polyline a smooth curve shape, you must use the Pedit command after you create the polyline.

The Explode command reduces a polyline to its line and arc components. Polylines with a width value lose their width once exploded.

See Also   Explode, Offset, Pedit

PLOT

● **VERSIONS**   All versions

● **PURPOSE**   Sends your drawing to a plotter. You can control the plotter pen selection and speed as well as where and how the drawing appears on the plotter media. Plot also allows AutoCAD to reduce a scale drawing to fit on the media. Once you change any of the plotter settings, they become the default settings.

To Plot a Drawing

- From the keyboard: **Plot⏎**
- From the screen menu: **Plot-Plot or Plotter**
- From the pull-down menu: **File-Plot**

Then follow these steps:

1. **What to plot—Display, Extents, Limits, View or Window <default>:** Enter the desired option. If View is chosen, you are prompted for a view name.

2. **Plot will not be written to a selected file**
    Sizes are in Inches
    Plot origin is at (0.00,0.00)
    Plotting area is 11.00 wide by 8.50 high (MAX size)
    Plot is NOT rotated
    Pen width is 0.010
    Area fill will NOT be adjusted for pen width
    Hidden lines will NOT be removed
    Plot will be scaled to fit available area

    Do you want to change anything? <N> Enter **Y** if you want to change the default plotter settings shown above. You will get a series of prompts that allow you to change the settings. If you enter **N**, you will skip to the **Write the plot to a file?** prompt.

3. **Write the plot to a file? <N>** Enter **Y** to create a plot file or press ↵ to plot the drawing.

4. **Size units (Inches or Millimeters) <I>:** Enter the unit equivalent of your drawing.

5. **Plot origin in Inches <0.00,0.00>:** Enter the location of the drawing origin in relation to the plotter origin in X and Y coordinates. The coordinate values should be in final plot size, not in drawing scale sizes.

6. **Enter the Size or Width,Height (in Inches) <MAX>:** Enter the desired sheet size (see Table 5). You can specify nonstandard sizes by entering them as X and Y coordinates.

7. **Rotate plot 0/90/180/270 <0>.** Enter the orientation of the plot if other than 0 degrees rotation. Versions before 11 will ask if you want to rotate the plot 90 degrees and will not rotate three-dimensional views.

Table 5: Standard values for plotting size

Size	Width	Height
A	10.50	8.00
MAX	11.00	8.50

8. **Pen width <0.010>:** Enter the pen width used for solid fills.

9. **Adjust area fill boundaries for pen width? <N>.** Enter **Y** if you want the plotter to compensate for pen width on solid filled areas. If you respond Y to this prompt, AutoCAD will offset the border of a filled area by half the pen width so that the area will accurately plot.

10. **Remove hidden lines? <N>** Enter **Y** if you want a three-dimensional view to be plotted with hidden lines removed.

11. **Specify scale by entering:**
    Plotted Inches=Drawing Units or Fit or ? <F>: Enter a scale factor for plot or **F** to force drawing to fit entirely on the sheet.

12. **Effective plotting area:** A value will appear showing you the width and height of the final plotted image. The size of the image will depend on the sheet size entered at the **Standard values for plotting size** prompt, plus the scale factor.

13. **Enter file name for plot <JUNK>:** If this prompt appears, enter the desired plot file name.

14. **Processing vector:** Numbers will appear as AutoCAD sends information to the plotter. **Plot complete. Press RETURN to continue:** Press ↵ to return to the drawing editor.

● **NOTES**   Since some plotters do not have built-in line types, the Select linetype option may not appear on your plotter.

If you respond Y to the **Write the plot to a file** prompt, AutoCAD creates a file on your disk to which it sends the plot information.

At the **Enter the size** prompt, the available sizes for your plotter are displayed. You can either enter one of these or a custom size.

The **Pen width** prompt works with the **Adjust fill** prompt, allowing your plotter to compensate for the pen width during area fills. If you respond with a Y at the **Adjust fill** prompt, AutoCAD uses the **Pen width** value to offset the outline of any filled areas to half the pen width. This causes the edge of filled areas to be drawn to the center line of the fill outline.

If you are using a laser printer, the **Pen width** value determines the thickness of a typical line.

You can also issue the Plot command from the AutoCAD Main menu as option 3, Plot a drawing.

At times, even though all of your plotter settings are correct, your plot may not appear in the proper location on your sheet, or the drawing may not be plotted at all. This often occurs when you are plotting the extents of a drawing. AutoCAD often does not recognize changes to the extents of the drawing when major portions of a drawing have been removed or edited. If you have this problem with a plot, open the file to be plotted and issue a Zoom/Extents. Let the drawing complete the regeneration process (it will probably regenerate twice), and try plotting again. If the problem persists, double-check your size units, plot origin, plot size, and plot scale settings.

If you have problems rotating a plot, use the UCS command to create a UCS that is rotated the way you want, and the View command to save a view of your drawing in the new UCS. Then use the View option under the **What to plot** prompt.

Version 11 users can plot from Paperspace. Such plots include all viewports and layer settings.

See Also   Prplot

POINT

● **VERSIONS**　All versions

● **PURPOSE**　Point draws a point entity. Points can be used as unobtrusive markers that you can snap to using the Node Osnap override.

Sequence of Steps

- From the keyboard: **Point⏎**

- From the screen menu: **Draw-next-Point**

Then complete the following step:

Point: Enter the point location.

● **OPTIONS**

You can set the Pdmode system variable to change the appearance of points. You must set Pdmode before drawing points. 0 is the default setting. When Pdmode is changed, all existing points are updated to reflect the new setting. The setting values are as follows:

0	A dot
1	Nothing
2	A cross
3	An x
4	A vertical line up from the point selected
32	A circle
64	A square

● **NOTES**　You can combine the different Pdmode variables to create 20 different types of points. For example, to combine a cross (2) with a circle (32), set Pdmode to 34 (2 + 32).

In version 11, you can set Pdmode and Pdsize through the Point
Size and Point Type options under the Options pull-down menu.

See Also   Divide, Measure, Pdmode, Pdsize

POINT SELECTION

- **VERSIONS**   All versions

- **PURPOSE**   You can enter a point by picking it with your cursor, keying in an absolute or relative coordinate value, or keying in
a relative polar coordinate. You can also use modifiers called filters
to align points in an X-, Y-, or Z-axis.

- **OPTIONS**

Absolute coordinate   Specifies points by giving the X, Y and Z
coordinate values separated by commas, as follows:

Select point: 6,3,1

The X value is 6, the Y is 3, and the Z is 1. If you omit the Z value,
AutoCAD assumes the current default Z value (see the Elev command to set the current Z default value). Absolute coordinates use
the current UCS's origin as the point of reference.

Relative coordinates   Entered like absolute coordinates, except
that an *at* sign (@) precedes the coordinate values, as follows:

Select point: @6,3,1

If you omit the Z value, AutoCAD assumes the current default Z value (see the **Elev** command for setting the current Z
default value). Relative coordinates use the last point entered as the
point of reference. To tell AutoCAD to use the last point selected,
simply enter the *at* sign by itself at a point selection prompt.

Relative polar coordinates Specify points by giving the distance from the last point entered, preceded by an *at* sign and followed by a *less-than* sign and the angle, as follows:

Select point: @6<45

This entry calls for a relative distance of 6 units at a 45-degree angle from the last point entered.

Spherical coordinate Specifies three-dimensional points by distance from the last point, angle from the X-axis, and the angle from the X-Y plane, as follows:

@3.5<45<30

Omit @ to specify an absolute coordinate. Spherical coordinates are only allowed in version 11.

Cylindrical coordinate Specifies three-dimensional points by their distance in the X-Y plane, angle from the X-axis, and distance in the Z-axis, as follows:

@5.0<30,6.6

Omit @ to specify an absolute coordinate. Cylindrical coordinates are only allowed in version 11.

Filters Align a point along an X-, Y-, or Z-axis by first specifying the axis on which to align, then selecting an existing point on which to align, and then entering the new point's remaining coordinate values. The following example aligns a point vertically on a specific X location:

Point: .x ↵

of <pick>: Select a known point to which you want to align vertically. For precision, use the Osnap overrides.

(need yz): Select Y-Z coordinate. Again, you can use Osnap overrides to align to other geometries.

You can also enter **.xy**, **.yz**, or **.xz** at the **Point** prompt. For example, you can first pick an X-Y location then enter a Z value for height.

- **NOTES**   To override the current angle units, base, and direction settings (set using the Units command) use double or triple *greater-than* signs (<):

  <<   Enters angles in degrees, default angle base (east) and direction (counter clockwise) regardless of the current settings.

  <<<   Enters angles based on the current angle format (degrees, radians, grads, etc.), default angle base (east) and direction (counter clockwise), regardless of the base and direction settings.

In version 11, you can enter fractional units regardless of the unit style setting. This means you can enter **5.5**" as well as **5'6**" when using the architectural format.

See Also   Osnap, Units

POLYGON

- **VERSIONS**   2.5 and later

- **PURPOSE**   Allows you to draw a regular polygon of up to 1024 sides. To define the polygon, you can specify the outside or inside radius, or the length of one side. The polygon is actually a polyline that can be exploded into its individual component lines.

To Draw a Polygon

- From the keyboard: **Polygon**⏎
- From the screen menu: **Draw-next-Polygon**
- From the pull-down menu: **Draw-Polygon** (11)

Then follow these steps:

1. **Number of sides:** Enter the number of sides.

2. **Edge/<Center of polygon>:** Enter **E** to select **Edge** option or pick a point to select the polygon center. If you select the default center of a polygon, the following prompts appear: **Inscribed in circle/Circumscribed about circle (I/C):** Enter the desired option. **Radius of circle:** Enter the radius of circle defining polygon size.

● OPTIONS

Edge   Determines the length of one face of the polygon. You are prompted to select the first and second end point of the edge. AutoCAD then draws a polygon by creating a circular array of the edge you specify.

Inscribed   Forces the polygon to fit inside a circle of the specified radius; the end points of each line lie along the circumference.

Circumscribed   Forces the polygon to fit outside, or encompass, a circle of the specified radius; the midpoint of each line lies along the circumference.

Radius of circle   Sets the length of the defining radius of the polygon. The radius will be the distance from the center to either an endpoint or a midpoint, depending on the Inscribed/Circumscribed choice.

See Also   Pedit, Pline

PROJECT (AUTOLISP)

● VERSIONS   9 and later

● PURPOSE   Creates a two-dimensional drawing from a three-dimensional model. This is useful for producing working drawings, such as building elevations, from three-dimensional models.

Sequence of Steps

- From the keyboard: **(load "<drive>:/<path>/project")**⏎ **Project**⏎

- From the screen menu: **Bonus-next-Project**

Then follow these steps:

If you are using version 11, you will receive the following prompt:

   1. Enter projection type (1 or 2) <1>

If you are using versions 9 or 10, or if you are using version 11 and press ⏎ at step 2, you receive the following series of prompts:

   2. Layer name <current>: Enter the name of an existing layer you wish to place the projected drawing on.

   3. Select objects: Pick the objects on the three-dimensional model you wish to project. A message appears that either tells you to wait or states that AutoCAD was unable to project the selected objects. Next, the following prompt appears:

   4. Project another entity? Y/N <N>: Enter your choice. If AutoCAD was successful in projecting the objects you selected, the following prompts appear:

   5. Make into block? <N>: Enter **Y** to turn two-dimensional projection into a block.

   6. Write to disk as DWG file? <N>: Enter Y to write two-dimensional projection out as a drawing file.

• OPTIONS

If you are using version 11, and you enter 2 in response to step 1, the following series of prompts appears:

   UCS name or <RETURN> to select 3 points: Enter the name of the existing UCS or press ⏎ to define plane of projection.

From here, the prompts are the same as those beginning at step 2.

● **NOTES**   3D meshes cannot be projected without first exploding them into their component 3Dfaces. This includes objects created using Revsurf, Tabsurf, Edgesurf, and Rulesurf, as well as 3D objects such as cones, boxes, spheres, domes and dishes.

From the keyboard, you have to load Project only once per editing session. You can then use Project at any time. It is not necessary to load Project if you are using the menu.

See Also   AutoLISP

PRPLOT

● **VERSIONS**   2.0 and later

● **PURPOSE**   Sends your drawing to a dot matrix printer for hard copy output. All of the options are the same as for the Plot command, except the options related to pens.

To Print on a Dot Matrix Printer

- From the keyboard: **Prplot** ↵
- From the screen menu: **Plot-Print(er)**
- From the pull-down menu: **File-Print**
- From the main menu: **4** ↵

See Also   Plot

PSPACE

● **VERSIONS**   11

• **PURPOSE**   Lets you move from Modelspace to Paperspace.

Sequence of Steps

- From the keyboard: **Pspace**↵

- From the screen menu: **Mview-Pspace**

- From the pull-down menu: **Display-Mview-Pspace**

If the Tilemode system variable is set to 0, AutoCAD will switch to Paperspace. If it isn't, you receive the message:

** Command not allowed unless tilemode is set to 0 **

• **NOTES**   Paperspace is an alternative work space that lets you arrange views of your Modelspace drawing. Paperspace is a "paste up" area, independent from the main drawing (Modelspace).

You can create viewports in Paperspace that are like windows into Modelspace. Layers, Snap, and Grid modes can be set independently for each viewport. You can also accurately control the scale of a viewport for plotting purposes.

To get into Paperspace in a new drawing, set Tilemode to 0, then issue Pspace. Your screen will go blank and the UCS icon will change to an triangle. Use the Mview command to set up Viewports so you can display your Modelspace drawing in Paperspace. Use the Xp option under the Zoom command to set the scale of a viewport display.

Viewports in Paperspace can be resized, moved, copied, and even overlapped using standard AutoCAD editing commands.

See Also   Mspace, Mview, Mvsetup, Tilemode, Vplayer, Vports, Zoom/Xp

PTEXT (ADS, AutoLISP)

- **VERSIONS** 11

- **PURPOSE** Simplifies the input and editing of text para-
graphs. It has a word wrap capability and lets you control justification. The Edit option lets you edit text by placing a cursor on exact
text locations.

Sequence of Steps

- From the keyboard: **(load"<drive>: /<path> /ptext")**⏎
  Ptext⏎

- From the screen menu: **Bonus-next-Ptext**

Then complete the following step:

   Center/Edit/Fit/Right/Slack/?/<Start point>: Pick the start
   point for the text or enter an option.

- **OPTIONS**

Center/Right Controls the justification of the text. Center aligns
the text through the center of each line. Right justifies the text to the
right. You are prompted to pick a start point, then, the following
series of prompts appears:

1. **Text height <0.2000>:** Indicate the height of text.

2. **Rotation angle <0>:** Indicate the rotation angle.

3. **Inter-line spacing <0.3000>:** Indicate the line spacing.

4. **Maximum line length <7.0000>:** Indicate the maximum
    length of the line for word wrap.

5. **Text:** Enter text.

Edit Edits text created using Ptext. A cursor appears in the block
of text you select. Control characters move the cursor up, down,

left, and right. You can toggle insert and overwrite mode. When you select Edit, the following series of prompts appears:

Select the text for editing. Start with the first line of the paragraph, and select the lines in order...Select objects:

Select each line of text from top to bottom. Use the following control characters to maneuver in the selected text.

Ctrl-A	Append a space after the cursor location.
Ctrl-B	Move cursor to the beginning of a line.
Ctrl-D	Move the cursor down one line.
Ctrl-E	Move the cursor to the end of a line.
Ctrl-H	Delete the character to the left of the cursor.
Ctrl-I	Switch between Insert and overwrite mode.
Ctrl-L	Move the cursor to the left one character.
Ctrl-N	Move the cursor to the end of the paragraph.
Ctrl-R	Move the cursor to the right one character.
Ctrl-T	Move the cursor to the beginning of the paragraph.
Ctrl-U	Move the cursor up one line.
Ctrl-Z	Exit the Ptext command.
Ctrl-?	Display a list of control characters.
Ctrl-F1	Same as Ctrl-?
Delete	Delete a character.

Fit Forces the text to fit exactly in a specified width. The text is stretched horizontally while text height is maintained. You are prompted for a left and right baseline point, then the same series of prompts appear as for the Center and Right options, excluding the rotation angle.

Slack Sets the overrun tolerance for the length of a line of text.

? Displays a help message listing input modes and control characters.

● **NOTES**   There are two versions of Ptext: an AutoLISP version and an ADS application. When you pick Ptext from the Screen menu, AutoCAD searches the DOS path and AutoCAD environment settings to locate the ADS version. If this search fails, AutoCAD searches for the Autolisp version. The only difference between the two versions is that the ADS is faster.

Ptext requires use of the AutoCAD Handles function.

See Also   Dtext, Handles, Text

PURGE

● **VERSIONS**   2.0 and later. Version 11 added the Dimstyle option.

● **PURPOSE**   A drawing may accumulate unneeded blocks, layers, and other elements. These objects and settings can increase the size of the drawing file, making the drawing slow to load and difficult to transport. Purge allows you to eliminate these elements. You can only use this command as the first command after you open the file.

To Purge Elements from the Drawing File

• From the keyboard: **Purge**⏎

• From the screen menu: **Utility-Purge**, **Purge unused**, **Blocks/Dimstyles/LAyers/LTypes/SHapes/STyles/All:** Enter the option to purge from the file.

When you enter the variable type name at the **Purge** prompt, AutoCAD displays each variable name of the type specified. Enter a **Y** to purge the variable or **N** to keep it. The All option displays all variables, regardless of type.

● **NOTES**   Versions 10 and 11 allow you to use Purge later in an editing session, as long as you haven't made any changes to the drawing's database during that session. You can use commands that affect the display of the drawing and still use Purge afterward, but if you use a drawing or editing command, Purge is no longer accessible. You must close the file and reopen it to use the Purge command.

See Also   Wblock

QTEXT

● **VERSIONS**   2.0 and later

● **PURPOSE**   Helps reduce drawing regeneration and redraw times by making text appear as a rectangular box instead of readable text. The rectangle approximates the height and length of the text.

Sequence of Steps

- From the keyboard: **Qtext** ↵

- From the screen menu: **Settings-next-Qtext**

Then complete the following step:

ON/OFF <Off>: Enter the desired option.

● **NOTES**   Qtext forces a regeneration. If Regenauto is turned off, you do not see the effects of Qtext until you issue a Regen command.

See Also   Dtext, Ptext, Regen, Text

QUIT

- **VERSIONS** All versions

- **PURPOSE** Exits a drawing without saving the most recent edits. The file reverts to the condition it was in following the last Save or End command. If you pick **Quit** from the Utility menu the Quit menu appears. Quit is not issued until you pick **Yes** from the Quit menu. A *Yes* response is automatically entered at the **Really want to discard file** prompt, and you exit the drawing.

To Exit without Saving

- From the keyboard: **Quit** ↵

- From the screen menu: **Utility-Quit**

- From the pull-down menu: **File-Quit**

Then complete the following step:

Really want to discard all changes to drawing? Enter **Y** to exit or ↵ to abort the Quit command.

See Also End, Save

RADIUS (DIM)

- **VERSIONS** 2.0 and later

- **PURPOSE** Adds a radius dimension to arcs and circles.

Before Dimensioning

You must have issued the **Dim** or **Dim1** command to use any dimensioning subcommand.

To Add a Radius Dimension

- From the keyboard: **Radius** ↵

- From the screen menu: **Dim-radius** (9, 10), **Dim-radial-radius** (11)

Then follow these steps:

1. **Select arc or circle:** Pick the arc or circle. The point at which you pick the arc or circle determines one end of the dimension arrow.

2. **Dimension text <default radius>:** Press ↵ to accept the default radius or enter text.

3. **Enter leader length for text:** Pick a point indicating the leader length.

- **NOTES**   For version 10 and earlier, step 3 does not occur. Also, if the arc or circle is too small, the following prompt appears:

    Text does not fit.
    Enter leader length for text: Pick a point representing the length of the text leader or enter a value.

A leader line is drawn from the selection point at the length specified. The direction from the center point to the pick point determines the direction of the leader. A center mark is also placed at the center of the arc or circle.

- **See Also**   Dimension Variable: Dimcen

RECOVER DAMAGED DRAWINGS

● **VERSIONS**   11

● **PURPOSE**   A drawing may become corrupted because of problems with your hard disk drive or floppy disk. Corrupted files cannot be opened by AutoCAD. Recover salvages as much of a file as possible and allows AutoCAD to read the file.

To Recover Corrupted Files

1.   Go to the AutoCAD main menu.

2.   Enter **9** at the **Enter selection** prompt.

3.   Enter the name of the corrupted file at the **Enter name of file** prompt.

4.   A series of messages appears indicating the action AutoCAD is taking to recover the file.

● **NOTES**   AutoCAD will not recover files from earlier versions.

See Also   Command: Audit

RECTANG (AUTOLISP)

● **VERSIONS**   11

● **PURPOSE**   Simplifies the drawing of a rectangle.

Sequence of Steps

- From the keyboard: **(load "<drive>:/<path>/rectang")** ↵
  rectang ↵

- From the screen menu: **Bonus-next-Rectang**

Then follow these steps:

1. **Corner of rectangle or square:** Pick the first corner of
   the rectangle.

2. **Length:** Indicate the X-axis length.

3. **Square/<Width>:** Indicate the Y-axis length or enter **S** for
   a square.

A polyline rectangle will be drawn.

● **NOTES**   From the keyboard, you have to load Rectang only
once per editing session. You can then use Rectang at any time. It is
not necessary to load Rectang if you are using the menu.

See Also   Commands: Pedit, Pline, Polygon

REDEFINE/UNDEFINE

● **VERSIONS**   9 and later

● **PURPOSE**   Undefine suppresses any standard AutoCAD command in favor of an AutoLISP program of the same name. For example, if you load the AutoLISP Copy command and enter **Copy** at
the **Command** prompt, you get the standard Copy command.
However, if you use Undefine to suppress the standard Copy command, you can use the AutoLISP Copy program. Redefine reinstates
a standard command that has been suppressed.

To Suppress or
Reinstate a Standard Command

• From the keyboard: **Undefine** ↵ or **Redefine** ↵

Then complete the following step:

Command name: Enter the command name.

● **NOTES**   To enter the standard AutoCAD Copy command, key
in a period in front of the command at the **Command** prompt, as
follows:

Command: .Copy ↵
Select objects:
.
.
.

This is the only way to issue an undefined command with the
AutoLISP Command function.

REDO

● **VERSIONS**   2.5 and later

● **PURPOSE**   Redo restores a command you have undone using
U or Undo. You are only allowed one Redo per command.

Sequence of Steps

• From the keyboard: **Redo** ↵

• From the screen menu: **Edit-next-Undo-Redo**

See Also   U, Undo

REDRAW AND REDRAWALL

● **VERSIONS**   All versions for Redraw. Versions 10 and 11 for Redrawall.

● **PURPOSE**   During the drawing and editing process, an operation may cause an object to partially disappear. Often, the object was previously behind other objects that have been removed. Redraw and Redrawall refresh the screen and restore such obscured objects. These commands also clear the screen of blips that may clutter your view.

Redraw will act only on the currently active viewport. Redrawall, on the other hand, refreshes all viewports on the screen at once. These commands affect only the virtual screen, not the actual drawing database.

To Refresh the Screen

- From the keyboard: '**Redraw** ↵ or '**Redrawall** ↵

- From the screen menu: **Display-Redraw** or **Redrawall**

- From the pull-down menu: **Tools-Redraw** (9), **Display-Redraw** (10, 11)

● **NOTES**   Redraw and Redrawall are transparent commands. When you pick them from the menu system or, from the keyboard, precede the command with an apostrophe, you can use them within other commands.

See Also   Commands: Regen, Viewres

REGEN AND REGENALL

● **VERSIONS**   All versions for Regen. Version 10 and 11 for Regenall.

● **PURPOSE**   Updates the drawing editor screen to reflect the most recent changes in the drawing database.

Sequence of Steps

- From the keyboard: **Regen** ↵ or **Regenall** ↵
- From the screen menu: **Display-Regen** or **Regenall**

● **NOTES**   If you make a global change in the drawing database and Regenauto is turned on, a regeneration is issued automatically. For example, zooming or panning into an area outside the virtual screen causes regeneration. Restoring a saved view that extends outside the virtual screen also causes a regeneration.

If you have Regenauto turned off, regeneration will not occur automatically, so changes to the drawing database are not immediately reflected in the drawing you see. If you need to see those changes, use Regen to update the display.

If you are using multiple viewports, Regen affects only the active viewport. To regenerate all viewports at once, use Regenall.

See Also   Regenauto, Viewres

REGENAUTO

● **VERSIONS**   2.5 and later

● **PURPOSE**   Automatically regenerates screen display to reflect most recent drawing changes. For complex drawings regeneration can be very time-consuming. Regenauto enables you to turn off automatic regeneration. Regenauto is on by default.

Sequence of Steps

- From the keyboard: **Regenauto** ⏎

- From the screen menu: **Display-Regenauto**

Then complete the following step:

ON/OFF/ <current status>: Enter the desired status.

● **OPTIONS**

On   Causes the display to be automatically regenerated when required to reflect global changes in the drawing database. Your display will reflect all the most recent drawing changes.

Off   Suppresses the automatic regeneration of the display. This can save time when you are editing complex drawings. When a command needs to regenerate the drawing, a prompt allows you to decide whether or not to regenerate the display.

See Also   Commands: Regen, Viewres. System Variable: Regenmode

RENAME

● **VERSIONS**   2.0 and later

● **PURPOSE**   Renames any namable drawing element, such as a block, layer, line type, text style, etc.

Sequence of Steps

- From the keyboard: **Rename** ↵

- From the screen menu: **Utility-Rename**

Then complete the following step:

Block/LAyer/LType/Style/Ucs/VIew/VPort: Enter the type of drawing element to be renamed.

RESTORE (DIM)

● **VERSIONS**   11

● **PURPOSE**   Makes an existing dimension style the current default style.

Before Dimensioning

You must have issued the **Dim** or **Dim1** command to use any dimensioning subcommand.

To Use Restore

- From the keyboard: **Restore.**↵

- From the screen menu: **Dim-next-Restore**

Then follow these steps:

1. **Current dimension style: <Style_name> ?/Enter dimension style name or RETURN to select dimension:** Enter ? to list available dimension styles, or enter the name of a known dimension style, or press ↵ to pick a dimension whose dimension style you want to make current.

If you enter ?, you see the following prompt:

2. **Dimension style(s) to list <*>:** Enter a name specification. Wildcard characters are accepted.

After listing the dimension style names, AutoCAD returns to the prompt shown in step 2, allowing you to enter the name of a dimension style.

● **NOTES** To select a dimension style, either pick an associative dimension that is associated with the desired style, or enter the name of the style.

To find the differences between the current dimension style and another style, enter a dimension style name preceded with a tilde (~) at the prompt in step 2. Differences are displayed in a list of dimension variable settings.

See Also Save, Override, Wildcard characters

RESUME

See Script.

REVSURF

● **VERSIONS** 10, 11

● **PURPOSE** Draws an extruded curved surface that is rotated about an axis, like a bell, globe, or drinking glass (see Figure 19). Before you can use Revsurf, you must define both the shape of the extrusion and an axis of rotation. Use arcs, lines, circles, or two-dimensional or three-dimensional polylines to define this shape. The axis of rotation can be a line.

Sequence of Steps

- From the keyboard: **Revsurf** ⏎

- From the screen menu: **Draw-next-3D surfs-Revsurf**

- From the pull-down menu: **Draw-Surfaces-Surface of Revolution Icon**

Then follow these steps:

1. **Select path curve:** Pick an arc line, arc, circle, two-dimensional polyline, or three-dimensional polyline defining the shape to be swept.

2. **Select Axis of revolution:** Pick a line representing the axis of rotation.

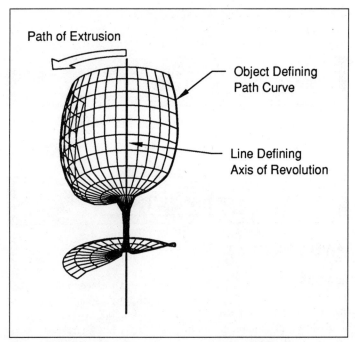

Figure 19: Extruded curved surface drawn by Revsurf

3. **Starting Angle <0>:** Enter the angle from the object selected as the path curve where the sweep starts.

4. **Included angle (+=ccw, –=cw) <Full circle>:** Enter the angle of the sweep.

● **NOTES** The point you pick on the object in step 2 determines the positive and negative directions of the rotation. You can use the "right-hand rule" illustrated in Figure 20 to determine the positive direction of the rotation. Imagine placing your thumb on the axis line, pointing away from the end closest to the pick point. The rest of your fingers will point in the positive rotation direction. The rotation direction determines the N direction of the surface while the axis of rotation defines the M direction.

You can control the number of facets used to create the revsurf by setting the Surftab1 and Surftab2 system variables. Surftab1 controls the number of facets in the M direction while Surftab2 controls the facets in the N direction. You can set these variables from the Surfaces Icon menu or through the Setvar command.

See Also Commands: Pedit, 3dmesh. System Variables: Splframe, Surftab1, Surftab2

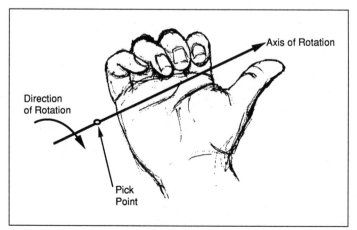

Figure 20: Determining the positive direction of rotation

ROTATE

- **VERSIONS**   2.5 and later

- **PURPOSE**   Rotates an object or group of objects to a specified angle.

Sequence of Steps

- From the keyboard: **Rotate** ↵

- From the screen menu: **Edit-next-Rotate**

- From the pull-down menu: **Modify-Rotate** (11)

Then follow these steps:

1. **Select objects:** Select as many objects as you like.

2. **Base point:** Pick the point about which objects are to be rotated.

3. **<Rotation angle>/Reference:** Enter the angle of rotation or **R** to specify a reference angle.

- **OPTIONS**

Reference   Allows you to specify the rotation angle in reference to the object's current angle. If you enter this option, you get the prompts:

Reference angle <0>: Enter the current angle of the object or pick two points representing a base angle.

New angle: Enter a new angle or pick an angle with the cursor.

ROTATED (DIM)

● **VERSIONS**   2.0 and later

● **PURPOSE**   Measures and places a dimension at a specified angle regardless of the dimensioned object's orientation. The dimension text is in the current text style. As illustrated in Figure 2, a rotated dimension measures a distance at the specified angle.

Before Dimensioning

You must have issued the Dim or Dim1 command to use any dimensioning subcommand.

To Rotate a Dimension

● From the keyboard: **Rotated** ↵

● From the screen menu: **Dim-Linear-Rotated**

Then follow these steps:

1. **First extension line origin or RETURN to select:** Pick one end of the object to be dimensioned.

2. **Second extension line origin:** Pick the other end of the object.

3. **Dimension line location:** Pick a point or enter a coordinate indicating the location of the dimension line.

4. **Dimension text:** <default dimension>: Press ↵ to accept the default dimension or enter a dimension value.

RPOLY (AUTOLISP)

- **VERSIONS**   10 and later

- **PURPOSE**   Generates a smooth convex polygon from a random polygon. It does this by repeatedly drawing new polygons. Each new polygon uses the midpoints of the previous polygon as its vertices.

Sequence of Steps

- From the keyboard: **(load "<drive>:/<path>/rpoly")** ↵ **rpoly** ↵

- From the screen menu: **Bonus-next-Rpoly**

Then follow these steps:

1. **First point:** Pick a beginning point for the random polygon.

2. **Next point:** Continue to pick points indicating the vertices of the random polygon. Press ↵ when you are done.

3. **Number of cycles:** Enter a number for the number of iterations of polygons you wish to generate.

4. **Retain polygon at each cycle <Y>/N:** Enter N if you want to keep only the first and last polygon generated.

- **NOTES**   From the keyboard, you have to load rpoly only once per editing session. You can then use rpoly at any time. It is not necessary to load Alias if you are using the menu.

See Also   Commands: Pedit, Polygon

RSCRIPT

See Script.

RULESURF

- **VERSIONS**   10

- **PURPOSE**   Generates a surface between two curves. Before
you can use Rulesurf, you must draw two curves defining opposite
ends of the desired surface (see Figure 21). The defining curves can
be points, lines, arcs, circles, two-dimensional polylines, or three-
dimensional polylines.

To Use Curves to Define a Surface

- From the keyboard: **Rulesurf** ↵

- From the screen menu: **3D-Rulesurf** (10), **Draw-next-3D
Surfs-Rulesurf** (11)

- From the pull-down menu: **Draw-3D Construction-Ruled
Surface icon** or **Draw-Surfaces-Ruled Surface icon**

Then follow these steps:

1. **Select first defining curve:** Enter the first curve.

2. **Select second defining curve:** Enter the second curve.

- **NOTES**   The location of your pick points on the defining
curves affects the way the surface is generated. If you want the surface to be drawn straight between the two defining curves, pick
points near the same position on each curve. If you want the surface

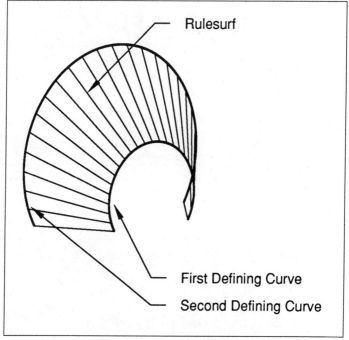

Rulesurf

First Defining Curve

Second Defining Curve

Figure 21: Defining the opposite ends of a surface for Rulesurf

to cross between the two defining curves, in a corkscrew fashion, pick points at opposite positions on the curves (see Figure 22).

The Surftab1 system variable controls the number of faces used to generate the surface.

See Also   Commands: Pedit. System Variables: Surftab1

SAVE

● **VERSIONS**   All versions

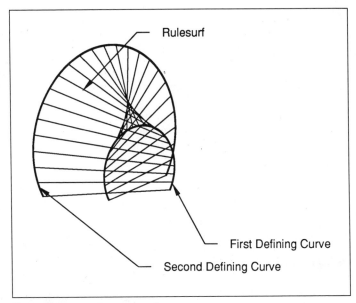

Figure 22: A corkscrew surface

● **PURPOSE**   Stores your currently open file to disk.

Sequence of Steps

- From the keyboard: **Save** ↵

- From the screen menu: **Save**

- From the pull-down menu: **File-Save**

Then complete the following step:

In version 11, a dialog box appears with a variety of options and a list of files (see Files Dialog Box). Other versions display the following prompt:

File name <Current file name>:

Enter the file name or press ↵ to accept the default current file name.

● **NOTES** It is a good idea to save your AutoCAD work to disk at 15 minute intervals to protect it against power outages or computer failures. You can use Save without closing the file or leaving the drawing editor.

If you enter a name that is different from the current file name you will create a new file that has the name you enter. The file will be a copy of the current file that has the changes made up to the time the Save command was issued. Entering a different name from the current file name does not change the current file name.

SAVE (DIM)

● **VERSIONS** 11

● **PURPOSE** Saves the current dimension variable settings as a dimension style that can later be restored using the Restore subcommand. You can save multiple dimension styles.

Before Dimensioning

You must have issued the **Dim** or **Dim1** command to use any dimensioning subcommand.

To Save Dimension Settings

- From the keyboard: **Save** ↵

- From the screen menu: **Dim-next-Save**

Then follow these steps:

1. **?/Name for new dimension style:** Enter a new dimension style name.

If you enter a name of an existing style, you get the following prompt:

2. **That name is already in use, redefine it? <N>** If you enter **Y** in response to this prompt, AutoCAD updates the specified style and all the dimensions that are associated with that style. If you enter **?**, the following prompt appears:

3. **Dimension styles to list<>:** Enter a name specification. Wildcards are accepted.

After listing the dimension style names, AutoCAD returns to the prompt shown in step 2, allowing you to enter the name of a dimension style.

● **NOTES**   The tilde (~) can also be used to compare styles.

To find the differences between the current dimension style and another style, enter a dimension style name preceded by a tilde (~) at the prompt in step 2. Differences are displayed in a list of dimension variable settings.

See Also   Override, Restore

SCALE

● **VERSIONS**   2.5 and later

● **PURPOSE**   Changes the size of objects in a drawing. You can also scale an object by reference.

Sequence of Steps

- From the keyboard: **Scale** ↲
- From the screen menu: **Edit-next-Scale**
- From the pull-down menu: **Modify-Scale** (11)

Then follow these steps:

1. **Select objects:** Pick the objects to be scaled.

2. **Base point:** Pick a point of reference for scaling.

3. **<Scale factor>/Reference:** Enter the scale factor, move the cursor to visually select new scale, or enter **R** to select the Reference option.

● **OPTIONS**

Reference Allows you to specify a scale in relation to a known length.

See Also Block, Insert, Select

SCRIPT

● **VERSIONS** All versions

● **PURPOSE** "Plays back" a set of AutoCAD commands and responses recorded in a Script file. Script files, like DOS batch files, are lists of commands and responses entered exactly as you would while in AutoCAD.

Sequence of Steps

● From the keyboard: **Script** ↵

● From the screen menu: **Utility-Script**

Then complete the following step:

Version 11 displays a files dialog box. Earlier versions display the following prompt:

Script file <current file name>:

Enter the script file name.

From the DOS prompt, you can start AutoCAD and a script at the same time by entering the following:

ACAD <drawing file name> <script file name>

● OPTIONS

Delay   When included in a Script file, makes AutoCAD pause for the number of milliseconds indicated.

Rscript   When included at the end of a Script file, repeats the script continuously.

Resume   Restarts a Script file that has been interrupted using the Backspace or Ctrl-C key.

Backspace or **Ctrl-C**   Interrupts the processing of a Script file.

● **NOTES**   You can use Script files to set up frequently used macros to save lengthy keyboard entries or to automate a presentation. Another common use for scripts is to automate plotter and printer setup.

When using a script from the DOS prompt, include the keystrokes you would enter at the main menu. For example, to plot a drawing from a script, key in **3** as the first line of the Script file. On the next line, key in the name of the file to plot. For the rest of the Script file, key in the proper responses to all of the plotter prompts.

SELECT

● **VERSIONS**   2.5 and later

● **PURPOSE**   Provides a variety of options for selecting objects and returns you to the **Command** prompt when you have made a selection. The objects selected become the most recent selection in AutoCAD's memory.

To Select Objects

- From the keyboard: **Select** ⏎

- From the screen menu: **Edit-Select**

Then complete the following step:

Select objects: Use the usual selection options to select objects to be edited later.

● OPTIONS

Window   Selects objects completely enclosed by a rectangular window.

Crossing   Selects objects that cross through a rectangular window.

Previous   Selects last set of objects selected for editing. You can use Previous to pick the objects you have picked with Select when a later command prompts you to select objects. The Previous option is useful when you want several commands to process the same set of objects, as in a menu macro.

Last   Selects last object drawn or inserted.

Remove   Removes objects from the current selection of objects.

Add   Adds objects to the current selection of objects. You will usually use this option after you have issued the R option.

Multiple   Allows you to pick several objects at once before highlighting them and adding them to the current selection of objects.

Undo   Removes the most recently added object from current selection of objects.

BOX   Allows you to use either a crossing or standard window, depending on the orientation of your window pick points. If you pick points from right to left, you will get a crossing window. You will get a standard window if you pick points from left to right.

AUto   Allows you to select objects by picking them or by using a window, as you would with the Box option. After you issue the

AUto option, you can pick objects individually, as usual. If no object is picked, AutoCAD assumes you want to use the Box option, and a window appears that allows you to use either a crossing or standard window to select objects.

SIngle   Selects only the first picked object or the first group of windowed objects.

● **NOTES**   The Select command only maintains a selection set until you pick a different group of objects at another **Select object** prompt. Entering the AutoLISP command **(setq set1 (ssget))** at the **Command** prompt allows you to create a selection set that will be maintained for the duration of the current editing session. You are prompted to select objects. After you are done, you are returned to the **Command** prompt. Later, when you want to select this group of objects again, enter **!set1** at the **Select objects** prompt.

SETUP (AUTOLISP)

● **VERSIONS**   9 and 10 only

● **PURPOSE**   Establishes a drawing area based on your drawing scale and sheet size, as well as a unit style, such as architectural or decimal, based on the unit type you select. In version 11, setup is replaced by Mvsetup.

To Establish a Drawing Area

- From the keyboard: **(load "<drive>:/<path>/setup")**↵ **Setup** ↵

- From the screen menu: **Setup**

Then follow these steps:

1. **Select the units from the screen menu:** The menu displays a list of unit types available. Pick one.

2. **Select a scale from the screen menu:** The menu displays a list of scales available. Pick one.

3. **Select the paper size from the screen menu:** The menu displays a list of paper sizes available. Pick one or pick **VERTCAL>** if you want the sheet to be oriented vertically.

● OPTIONS

At the **Select a scale** prompt, you are presented with a set of predefined scales. Pick **Other** to enter a scale not shown on the menu. At the **Enter the scale:** prompt enter a single numeric value representing the desired scale. For example, for a scale of 1" equals 35', enter 420 (that is, 12" × 35').

At the **Select the paper size** prompt, select from a set of predefined paper sizes. To enter a paper size not shown on the menu, pick **Other**. The following prompts appear:

Enter the Horizontal Dimension of the paper:
Enter the Vertical Dimension of the paper:

Enter the desired paper size at each prompt.

When the setup is complete, a border is drawn marking the edges of the drawing sheet. This border represents the drawing limits (see Limits). Plotters usually place the drawing origin in the lower-left corner of the sheet, offset by the amount of the margin. Because most plotters leave a margin of approximately 3/8" around the drawing sheet, the border's top and right sides will not be plotted. You should draw another border inside the one provided by the Setup program and delete the original border.

● NOTES
From the keyboard, you have to load Setup only once per editing session. You can then use Setup at any time. It is not necessary to load Setup if you are using the menu.

See Also   Commands: Limits, Mvsetup, Units

SHADE

● **VERSIONS**   11

● **PURPOSE**   Produces a quick "Z buffer" shaded view of a 3D model. This command should not be confused with AutoShade, which is a separate program from AutoCAD.

To Quickly View a 3D Model

- From the keyboard: **Shade** ↵

- From the screen menu: **Display-Shade**

- From the pull-down menu: **Display-Shade**

The screen will go blank for a period of time while AutoCAD works to create the shaded image.

● **OPTIONS**

The Shadedge and Shadedif system variables give you some control over the way a model is shaded.

● **NOTES**   You can't plot images created using Shade. However, you can use the Slide command to store them for quick retrieval later.

On systems that support less than 256 colors, Shade produces an image with hidden lines removed and 3dfaces in their original color. However, Shade can produce an image faster than the Hide command, and might be used where speed is a consideration.

On systems with 256 colors or more, Shade produces a shaded image for which the light source and viewer location are the same.

See Also   System Variables: Shadedge, Shadedif

SHAPE

- **VERSIONS**   All versions

- **PURPOSE**   If you have created a group of custom shapes in an AutoCAD.SHX file, you can insert them using the Shape command. First, use the Load command to load the .SHX file. (AutoCAD provides a sample .SHX file called PC.SHX.) Shapes act like blocks, but you can't break them into their drawing components or attach attributes to them.

To Insert Custom Shapes

- From the keyboard: **Shape** ↵

- From the screen menu: **Draw-next-Shape**

Then follow these steps:

1. **Shape name (or ?) <default>:** Enter the name of the shape or a question mark to list available shapes.

2. **Start point:** Pick the insertion point.

3. **Height <1.0>:** Enter the height value or select a height using the cursor.

4. **Rotation angle <0.0>:** Enter or visually select the angle.

- **NOTES**   Since shapes take up less file space than blocks, you may want to use shapes in drawings that do not require the features offered by blocks.

See Also   Commands: Load, Wildcards

SHELL/SH

● **VERSIONS**   2.1 and later

● **PURPOSE**   Shell and Sh allow you to use any DOS command and run other programs with low memory requirements without exiting AutoCAD. Shell provides approximately 120K of RAM; Sh provides approximately 30K.

To Open a DOS Shell

• From the keyboard: **Shell** ↵ or **Sh** ↵

• From the screen menu: **Utility-External Commands-Shell** or **Sh**

Then complete the following step:

OS Command: Enter a standard DOS command or press ↵ to enter DOS.

● **NOTES**   If you want to use external DOS commands or programs, you must, before starting AutoCAD, either specify or set a path to the drive and directory where the commands or programs are located. Shell differs from Sh in that it allows the external commands to use larger amounts of memory.

If you press ↵ at the **OS command** prompt, the DOS prompt appears and you can enter any number of external commands. Key in **Exit** and press Enter to return to the AutoCAD **Command** prompt.

See Also   Command: Shroom.COM

SHROOM

- **VERSIONS**   11

- **PURPOSE**   Shroom is a stand-alone TSR (resident) program provided with AutoCAD that increases the size of the AutoCAD Shell.

Sequence of Steps

1. Make sure the file Shroom.COM is in the AutoCAD directory. If you installed AutoCAD in the normal way, it should be in the Samples directory along with a text document, Shroom.DOC, that describes how it works.

2. Before starting AutoCAD, enter Shroom at the DOS prompt. Shroom will automatically start AutoCAD.

3. Use the Shell command as described under Shell. You will see a message stating that AutoCAD is being swapped out.

- **OPTIONS**

Enter **Shroom -?** at the DOS prompt to see a help message on Shroom.

- **NOTES**   Shroom is a small (under 4K) resident program that frees nearly all the standard DOS memory during a Shell command. This means that you can run virtually any program you like under the Shell command.

See Also   Command: Shell

SKETCH

• **VERSIONS**   2.0 and later

• **PURPOSE**   Allows you to draw freehand. It actually draws short line segments end-to-end to achieve this effect. The lines Sketch draws are only temporary lines that show the path of the cursor. You must save the line through the Record and eXit options.

To Draw Freehand

• From the keyboard: **Sketch** ↵

• From the screen menu: **Draw-next-Sketch**

Then follow these steps:

1. **Record increment:** Enter a value representing the distance the cursor travels before a line is fixed along the sketch path.

2. **Pen eXit Quit Record Erase Connect:** Start your sketch line or enter an option.

• **OPTIONS**

Pen   As an alternative to the pick button on your pointing device, you can press **P** from the keyboard to toggle between the pen-up and pen-down modes. With the pen down, short temporary line segments are drawn as you move the cursor. With the pen up, no lines are drawn.

eXit   Saves any temporary sketch lines and then exits the Sketch command.

Quit   Exits the Sketch command without saving temporary lines.

Record   Saves temporary sketched lines while in the middle of the Sketch command.

Erase   Erases temporary sketched lines.

Connect   Allows you to continue from the end of a sketch line.

. (period) Allows you to draw a long line segment while in the Sketch command. With the pen up, place the cursor at the location of the long line segment, then press period.

● **NOTES**   To draw polylines with Sketch instead of standard lines, use the Setvar command to set the Skpoly system variable to 1, or select **Skpoly** from the Sketch menu before you start your sketch.

The easiest way to use Sketch is with a digitizer equipped with a stylus. You can trace over other drawings or photographs and refine them later. The stylus gives a natural feel to your tracing.

The **Record increment** prompt allows you to set the distance the cursor travels before AutoCAD places a line. The Record increment value can greatly affect the size of your drawing. If this value is too high, the sketch line segments are too apparent and your sketched lines will appear "boxy." If the increment is set too low, your drawing file becomes quite large, and regeneration and redrawing times increase dramatically. A rule of thumb is to set the Record increment value so that at least four line segments are drawn for the smallest 180-degree arc you anticipate drawing.

When AutoCAD runs out of RAM in which to store the lines being sketched it must pause for a moment to set up a temporary file on your disk drive to continue to store the sketch lines. Your computer will then beep and display the message **Please raise the pen.** If this occurs, press **P** to raise the pen. You may have to press **P** twice. When you get the message

Thank you. Lower the pen and continue

press **P** again to proceed with your sketch. Setting **Record increment** to a low value increases your likelihood of running out of RAM.

Turn the Snap and Ortho modes off before starting a sketch. Otherwise, the sketch lines will be forced to the snap points, or drawn vertically or horizontally. The results of having the Ortho mode on may not be apparent until you zoom in on a sketch line.

If you prefer, you can sketch an object and then use the Pedit/Fit command to smooth the sketch lines.

See Also   Commands: Pedit, Pline. System Variables: Sketchinc, Skpoly

SLIDELIB.EXE

● **VERSIONS**   9 and later

● **PURPOSE**   Slidelib.EXE is an external AutoCAD program that runs independently from AutoCAD. Use it to combine several slide files into a slide library file. You use slide libraries to create icon menus and to help organize slide files.

Sequence of Steps

•   At the DOS prompt, enter the following: **Slidelib slide-library-name < ascii-list** ⏎

● **NOTES**   Before you can create a slide library, you must create an ASCII file containing a list of slide file names to include in the library. Do not include the .SLD extension in the list of names. You can give the list any name and extension. You can then issue the Slidelib program from the DOS prompt.

See Also   Commands: Mslide, Vslide

SNAP

● **VERSIONS**   All versions

• **PURPOSE**   Controls the settings for the Snap mode. The Snap mode allows you to accurately place the cursor by forcing it to move in specified increments.

Sequence of Steps

• From the keyboard: **Snap** ↵

• From the screen menu: **Settings-next-Snap**

Then complete the following step:

Snap spacing or ON/OFF/Aspect/Rotate/Style
<default spacing>: Enter the desired snap spacing or an option.

• **OPTIONS**

Snap spacing   Allows you to enter the desired snap spacing. The Snap mode is turned on and the new snap settings take effect.

ON   Turns on the Snap mode. Has the same effect as pressing the F9 function key or the Ctrl-B keys.

OFF   Turns off the Snap mode. Has the same effect as pressing the F9 function key or the Ctrl-B keys.

Aspect   Enters a Y-axis snap spacing different from the X-axis snap spacing.

Rotate   Rotates the snap points and the AutoCAD cursor to an angle other than 0 and 90 degrees.

Style   Allows you to choose between the standard orthogonal snap style and an isometric snap style.

• **NOTES**   You can use the Rotate option to rotate the cursor; the Ortho mode will conform to the new cursor angle. This option also allows you to specify a snap origin, allowing you to accurately place hatch patterns. The Snapang system variable also lets you rotate the cursor.

If you use the Isometric style option, you can use the Isoplane command to control the cursor orientation. Also, the Ellipse command allows you to draw isometric ellipses.

You can set many of the settings available in the Snap command by using the Ddrmodes dialog box.

See Also   Commands: Ddrmodes, Ellipse, Hatch, Isoplane. System Variables: Snapang, Snapbase, Snapisopair, Snapmode, Snapunit

SOLID

- **VERSIONS**   All versions

- **PURPOSE**   Solid allows you to fill an area solidly. You determine the area by picking points in a crosswise, or "bow tie" fashion. Solid is best suited to filling in rectilinear areas. Polylines are better for filling in curved areas.

To Fill an Area

- From the keyboard: **Solid** ⏎
- From the screen menu: **Draw-next-Solid**

Then follow these steps:

1. **First point:** Pick one corner of the area to be filled.

2. **Second point:** Pick the next adjacent corner of the area.

3. **Third point:** Pick the corner diagonal to the last point selected.

4. **Fourth point:** Pick the next adjacent corner of the area.

Continue to pick points until you have defined the filled area. The **Third point** and **Fourth point** prompts appear as you continue to pick points.

• **NOTES**   In large drawings that contain many solids, you can reduce regeneration and redrawing times by setting the Fill command to Off until you are ready to plot the final drawing.

See Also   Commands: Fill, Pline, 3dface, Trace

SPIRAL (AUTOLISP)

• **VERSIONS**   9 and later

• **PURPOSE**   Draws a spiral.

Sequence of Steps

- From the keyboard: **(load "<drive>:/<path>/spiral")** ⏎
  Spiral ⏎

- From the screen menu: **Bonus-next-Spiral**

Then follow these steps:

1.   **Center point:** Pick the center of the spiral.

2.   **Number of rotations:** Enter a number.

3.   **Growth per rotation:** Indicate a distance between each spiral rotation.

4.   **Points per rotation <30>:** Enter a number indicating the number of facets for each rotation.

• **NOTES**   From the keyboard, you have to load Spiral only once per editing session. You can then use Spiral at any time. It is not necessary to load Spiral if you are using the menu.

SSX (AUTOLISP)

- **VERSIONS**   9 and later

- **PURPOSE**   Allows you to select objects by their properties.

Sequence of Steps

- From the keyboard: **(load "<drive>:/<path>/ssx")** ↵ **ssx** ↵

- From the screen menu: **Bonus-next-SSX**

Then follow these steps:

Version 11 users next see the prompt in step 1. Version 9 and 10 users skip to the prompt in step 2.

1. **Select object/<None>:** Pick an object or press ↵ to view options. If you pick an object, you will get a list of properties in the Autolisp list format.

2. **Blockname/Color/Entity/Flag/LAyer/LType/Pick/ Style/Thickness/Vector:** Enter the category by which objects are to be selected or filtered.

- **NOTES**   To use SSX at the **Select objects** prompt, enter SSX enclosed in parentheses, like this: (SSX). After you have entered a category at the **SSX** prompt, you remain at the prompt until you press ↵. You are then returned to the **Select objects** prompt with the objects fitting the SSX selection categories highlighted.

If you use SSX at the **Command** prompt, the objects selected become the most recent selection set, which you can act upon by using the Previous option from the Select objects prompt. Otherwise, you can use Ssx directly from the Select objects prompt to add objects to the current selection set.

From the keyboard, you have to load SSX only once per editing session. You can then use SSX at any time. It is not necessary to load SSX if you are using the menu.

See Also AutoLISP. Commands: Select

STATUS

● **VERSIONS** All versions

● **PURPOSE** Displays the current settings of a drawing, including the drawing limits and the status of all drawing modes. It also displays the current memory usage.

To Display Current Drawing Settings

• From the keyboard: **Status** ↵

• From the screen menu: **Inquiry-Status**

• From the pull-down menu: **Utility-Status**

You will see the display shown in Figure 23.

```
Loading acad.lsp...loaded.
Loaded menu C:\ACAD\SUPPORT\ACAD.mnx

Command: status
1919 entities in SITE-3D
Model space limits are X:      0'-0"   Y:      0'-0"  (Off)
                       X:      1'-0"   Y:      0'-9"
Model space uses       X:  -251'-7 3/4"  Y: -184'-1 1/2" **Over
                       X:   131'-1"   Y:  102'-8 1/4" **Over
Display shows          X:  -298'-11 3/4"  Y: -305'-9 1/4"
                       X:   204'-1"   Y:  160'-11 1/2"
Insertion base is      X:      0'-0"   Y:      0'-0"  Z:      0'-0"
Snap resolution is     X:      0'-1"   Y:      0'-1"
Grid spacing is        X:      0'-0"   Y:      0'-0"

Current space:         Model space
Current layer:         WALLS
Current color:         BYLAYER -- 7 (white)
Current linetype:      BYLAYER -- CONTINUOUS
Current elevation:      50'-0"  thickness:      0'-0"
Axis off  Fill on  Grid off  Ortho off  Qtext off  Snap off  Tablet off
Object snap modes:     None

Free disk: 292864 bytes
-- Press RETURN for more --
```

Figure 23: Drawing status display

```
-- Press RETURN for more --
Virtual memory allocated to program: 3368K
Amount of program in physical memory/Total (virtual) program size: 71%
Total conventional memory: 280K      Total extended memory: 4736K
Swap file size: 388K bytes
Page faults: 73     Swap writes: 0    Swap reclaims: 0
Command:
```

Figure 23: Drawing status display (cont'd)

● **NOTES**   There are some differences between the Status display of AutoCAD 386 and the standard DOS version, particularly with respect to the memory information. The following describes the 386 memory values:

Virtual memory allocated to program shows the amount of memory AutoCAD has taken.

Amount of program in physical memory/Total (virtual) program size shows the ratio of physical memory and virtual program size. A value of less than 100 indicates that some of the AutoCAD program has been paged to disk.

Total conventional memory shows the amount of standard DOS memory (640K) available to AutoCAD.

Total extended memory shows the total extended memory available to AutoCAD.

Swap file size shows the current size of the swap file.

Page faults: #   Swap writes: #   Swap reclaims: # shows swap file activity. Check these values frequently during an editing session to get an idea of how often AutoCAD must swap program information to the disk drive. If these values are high toward the end of your editing session, you may want to consider adding more RAM to your computer.

Modelspace limits and **Modelspace uses** change to **Paperspace limits** and **Paperspace uses** when you are in the Paperspace mode.

See Also   Layers, Settings, Time

STATUS (DIM)

- **VERSIONS**   1.4 and later

- **PURPOSE**   Displays the current Dimension variable settings and descriptions.

Before Dimensioning

You must have issued the **Dim** or **Dim1** command to use any dimensioning subcommand.

To Display Dimension Settings

- From the keyboard: **Status** ⏎

- From the screen menu: **Dim-Status**

Then follow these steps:

1. A list of current Dimension variable settings appears along with brief descriptions. When the list pauses, the following line appears: ---**Press RETURN for more**---

2. Press ⏎ to continue viewing the list or Ctrl-C to abort the command.

See Also   Dimension Variable: Dimsen

STRETCH

- **VERSIONS**   2.5 and later

- **PURPOSE**   Moves vertices of objects. Maintains the continuity of connected lines while moving objects.

Sequence of Steps

- From the keyboard: **Stretch** ↵

- From the screen menu: **Edit-next-Stretch**

- From the pull-down menu: **Edit-Stretch** (9), **Modify-Stretch** (10, 11)

Then follow these steps:

1. **Select objects:** Enter **C** to use a crossing window.

2. **Select objects:** Enter **R** to remove objects from the set of selected objects or press ↵ to confirm your selection.

3. **Base point:** Pick the base reference point for the stretch.

4. **New point:** Pick the second point in relation to the base point indicating the distance and direction you wish to move.

● **NOTES**   You can select vertex locations separately from the objects to be stretched. Indicate the vertices with a window, then select the objects individually with a pick. If there are several lines or other objects connected at the same vertex, use this method to stretch a selection of them.

Another way to use Stretch is to enter **C** (for crossing window) at the **Select objects** prompt. You can then deselect objects with the **Remove object** selection option. Do not use a window to deselect an object.

You cannot stretch blocks and text. If a block's or text's insertion point is included in a crossing window, the entire block will be moved.

See Also   Commands: Copy, Move

STYLE

● **VERSIONS**   2.0 and later

• **PURPOSE** Allows you to create a text style by specifying the AutoCAD font on which it is based, its height, its width factor, and the obliquing angle. You can change a font to be backwards, upside down, or vertical. See Figure 24 for a list of the standard AutoCAD fonts and Figure 25 for tables of the symbol, Greek, and Cyrillic fonts. You can also use Style to modify an existing text style.

To Create a Text Style

• From the keyboard: **Style** ⏎

• From the screen menu: **Settings-next-Style**

Then follow these steps:

1. **Text style name (or ?) <current style>:** Enter a style name or a question mark for a list of available styles. Wildcards are accepted with version 11.

Version 11 displays a files dialog box. Earlier versions display the following prompt:

2. **Font file <default font file>:** Enter a font file name or ⏎ to accept the default.

3. **Height <default height>:** Enter the desired height or ⏎ to accept the default.

4. **Width factor <default width factor>:** Enter the desired width factor or ⏎ to accept the default.

5. **Obliquing angle <default angle>:** Enter the desired width obliquing angle or ⏎ to accept the default.

6. **Backwards? <N>:** Enter Y if you want the text to read backward or ⏎ to accept N, the default.

7. **Upside-down? <N>:** Enter Y if you want the text to read upside down or ⏎ to accept N, the default.

8. **Vertical? <N>:** Enter Y if you want the text to read vertically or ⏎ to accept N, the default.

AutoCAD Font	Font Description
This is Txt	(Old version of Roman Simplex)
This is Monotxt	(Old version of Roman Complex)
This is Simplex	(Old version of Italic Complex)
This is Complex	
This is Italic	(Roman Simplex)
This is Romans	(Roman double stroke)
This is Romand	(Roman Complex)
This is Romanc	(Roman triple stroke)
This is Romant	
This is Scripts	(Script Simplex)
This is Scriptc	(Script Complex)
This is Italicc	(Italic Complex)
This is Italict	(Italic triple stroke)
Τηισ ισ Γρεεκσ	(This is Greeks — Greek Simplex)
Τηισ ισ Γρεεκχ	(This is Greekc — Greek Complex)
Узит ит Висиллив	(This is Cyrillic — Alphabetical)
Тхис ис Чйрилтлч	(This is Cyriltlc — Transliteration)
This is Gothice	(Gothic English)
This is Gothicg	(Gothic German)
This is Gothici	(Gothic Italian)

Figure 24: The AutoCAD script fonts

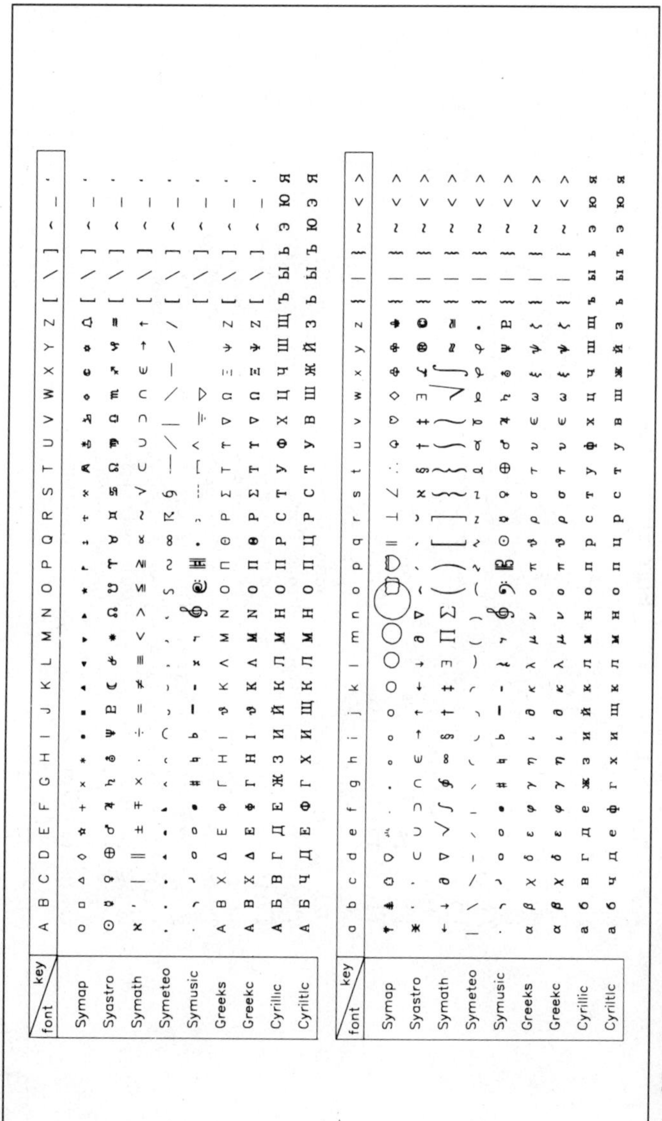

Figure 25: The AutoCAD symbol fonts

• OPTIONS

Text style name   Allows you to either enter a new name to define a new style or the name of an existing style to redefine the style.

Font file   Allows you to choose from several fonts. You can select from a set of predefined fonts from the Styles/Fonts menu or from the Fonts icon menu found on the Options pull-down menu. Version 11 users can select font files from a dialog box.

Height   Allows you to determine a fixed height for the style being defined. A 0 value allows you to determine text height as it is entered.

Width factor   Allows you to make the style appear expanded or compressed.

Obliquing angle   Allows you to "italicize" the style.

Backwards   Allows you to make the style appear backwards.

Upside down   Allows you to make the style appear upside down.

Vertical   Allows you to make the style appear vertical.

• NOTES   If you modify a style's font, text previously entered in that style is updated to reflect the modification. If any other style option is modified, previously entered text is not affected. Once you use the Style command, the style created or modified becomes the new current style.

A 0 value at the **Height** prompt causes AutoCAD to prompt you for a text height whenever you use this style with the Dtext and Text commands.

At the **Width factor** prompt, a value of 1 generates normal text. A greater value expands the style; smaller value compresses it.

At the **Obliquing angle** prompt, a value of 0 generates normal text. A greater value slants the style to the right, creating italics. A negative value slants the style to the left.

If you pick **Fonts** from the Options pull-down menu, a set of icon menus appear. These display the various standard fonts available (see Figure 26). When you pick a font from an icon menu, AutoCAD

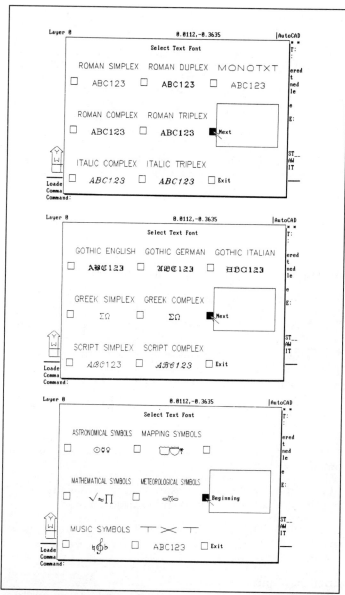

Figure 26: The Fonts icon menus

automatically enters a style name and font at the first two prompts. You enter the style height, width factor, obliquing angle, and so on.

See Also   Commands: Change, Dtext, Qtext, Text, Wildcards

STYLE (DIM)

- **VERSIONS**   1.4 and later

- **PURPOSE**   Specifies a text style for the dimension text. Once the text style is changed, any subsequent dimensions contain text in the new style. Existing dimension text is not affected.

Before Dimensioning

You must have issued the **Dim** or **Dim1** command to use any dimensioning subcommand.

To Specify a Text Style

1.   **Dim:** Style ⏎

2.   **New text style <current style>:** Press ⏎ to accept the current style or enter a new style name. The new style is now the current text style.

3.   If you enter the name of a style that does not exist, you receive the message: **No such text style.** Use the main Style command to create it.

See Also   Style. Dimension Variable: Dimtxt

SYSTEM VARIABLES/SETVAR

- **VERSIONS**   2.5 and later

- **PURPOSE**   The system variables control AutoCAD's many settings. Many of these variables are accessible through the commands they are associated with. At times, however, you will want to use the Setvar command to read or change them while you are in another command. You can do this because Setvar is a transparent command. You can issue it at any time by entering '**Setvar**. You can also access system variables through the AutoLISP interpreter with the Setvar and Getvar AutoLISP functions. Version 11 users can enter the system variable name directly at the command prompt.

To Set a System Variable

- From the keyboard: '**Setvar** ⏎

- From the screen menu: **Settings-next-Setvar**

Then complete the following step:

Variable name or ?: Enter the desired system variable name or a question mark for a list of variables.

- **OPTIONS**

Table 6 lists all of the system variables that you can access through Setvar. They fall into three categories: adjustable variables, read-only variables, and variables accessible only through Setvar. You can set an adjustable variable by issuing the Setvar command and the name of the desired variable. A prompt asks for an integer value. The meaning of that value depends on the nature of the variable. Version 11 users can enter the system variable name directly instead of using the Setvar command. System variable names can be used transparently by preceding the name with an apostrophe.

Table 6: System Variables

Adjustable Variables

You can adjust these variables either through the Setvar command or through the commands associated with the variable. For example, you can adjust the first three variables using the Units command, as well as Setvar.

Aflags — Controls the attribute mode settings: 1 = invisible, 2 = constant, 4 = verify, 8 = preset. For more than one setting, use the sum of the desired settings. See Attdef.

Angbase — Controls the direction of the 0 angle. Can also be set with the Units command.

Angdir — Controls the positive direction of angles: 0 = counterclockwise, 1 = clockwise. Can also be set with the Units command.

Aperture — Controls the Osnap cursor target height in pixels. Can also be set with the Aperture command.

Attmode — Controls the attribute display mode: 0 = off, 1 = normal, 2 = on. Can also be set with the Attdisp command.

Aunits — Controls angular units: 0 = decimal degrees, 1 = degrees-minutes-seconds, 2 = grads, 3 = radians, 4 = surveyors' units. Can also be set with the Units command.

Auprec — Controls the precision of angular units determined by decimal place. Can also be set with the Units command.

Axismode — Controls the axis mode: 0 = off, 1 = on. Can also be set with the Axis command.

Axisunit — Controls the X- and Y- axis spacing. Can also be set with the Axis command.

Blipmode — Controls the appearance of blips: 0 = off, 1 = on. See Blipmode.

Table 6: System Variables (cont'd)

Adjustable Variables	
Chamfera	Controls first chamfer distance. See Chamfer.
Chamferb	Controls second chamfer distance. See Chamfer.
Coords	Controls coordinate readout: 0 = coordinates are displayed only when points are picked. 1 = absolute coordinates are dynamically displayed as cursor moves. 2 = distance and angle are displayed during commands that accept relative distance input. Also controlled by the F6 function key.
Dragmode	Controls dragging: 0 = no dragging, 1 = on if requested, 2 = automatic drag. See Dragmode.
Elevation	Controls current three-dimensional elevation. See Elev.
Filletrad	Controls fillet radius. See Fillet.
Fillmode	Controls fill status: 0 = off, 1 = on. See Fill.
Gridmode	Controls grid: 0 = off, 1 = on. See Grid.
Gridunit	Controls grid spacing. See Grid.
Insbase	Controls insertion base point of current drawing. See Base.
Limcheck	Controls limit checking: 0 = no checking, 1 = checking. See Limits.
Limmax	Controls the coordinate of drawing's upper-right limit. See Limits.
Limmin	Controls the coordinate of drawing's lower-left limit. See Limits.
Ltscale	Controls the line type scale factor. See Ltscale.
Lunits	Controls unit styles: 1 = scientific, 2 = decimal, 3 = engineering, 4 = architectural, 5 = fractional. See Units.

Table 6: System Variables (cont'd)

Adjustable Variables	
Luprec	Controls unit accuracy by decimal place or size of denominator. See Units.
Orthomode	Controls the Ortho mode: 0 = off, 1 = on. See Ortho.
Osmode	Sets the current default Osnap mode: 0 = none, 1 = end point, 2 = midpoint, 4 = center, 8 = node, 16 = quadrant, 32 = intersection, 64 = insert, 128 = perpendicular, 256 = tangent, 512 = nearest, 1024 = quick. If more than one mode is required, enter the sum of those modes. See Osnap.
Qtextmode	Controls the Quick text mode: 0 = off, 1 = on. See Qtext command.
Regenmode	Controls the Regenauto mode: 0 = off, 1 = on. See Regenauto.
Sketchinc	Controls the sketch record increment. See Sketch.
Snapang	Controls snap and grid angle. See Snap.
Snapbase	Controls snap, grid, and hatch pattern origin. See Snap.
Snapisopair	Controls isometric plane: 0 = left, 1 = top, 2 = right. See Snap command.
Snapmode	Controls snap toggle: 0 = off, 1 = on. See Snap command.
Snapstyl	Controls snap style: 0 = standard, 1 = isometric. See Snap.
Snapunit	Controls snap spacing given in x and y values. See Snap.
Textsize	Controls default text height. See Dtext, Text, and Style.

Table 6: System Variables (cont'd)

Adjustable Variables	
Thickness	Controls three-dimensional thickness of objects being drawn. See Elev.
Tracewid	Controls trace width. See Trace.

Read-only Variables	
You can read these variables either through their associated commands or through Setvar. Rather than setting or adjusting some parameter of a drawing or of your AutoCAD system, they simply display the specified information.	
Acadver	Displays the AutoCAD version number.
Area	Displays the current area being computed. See Area.
Backz	Displays the distance from the Dview target to the back clipping plane. See Dview.
Cdate	Displays calendar date/time read from DOS. See Time.
Cecolor	Displays current object color. See Color.
Celtype	Displays current object line type. See Linetype.
Clayer	Displays current layer. See Layer and Ddlmode.
Date	Displays Julian date/time. See Time.
Distance	Displays last distance read using Dist. See Dist.
Dwgname	Displays drawing name. See Status.
Frontz	Displays the distance from the Dview target to the front clipping plane. See Dview.
Handles	Displays the status of the Handles command. 0 = off, 1 = on. See Handles.

Table 6: System Variables (cont'd)

Read-only Variables	
Lastangle	Displays the end angle of last arc or line. See Pline/Length.
Lastpoint	Displays coordinates of last point entered. Same point referenced by at sign (@).
Lenslength	Displays the current lens focal length used during the Dview command Zoom option.
Menuname	Displays the current menu file name. See Menu.
Perimeter	Displays the perimeter value currently being read by Area, List, or Dblist. See Area, List, or Dblist.
Popups	Displays the availability of the Advanced User Interface. 0 = not available, 1 = available.
Target	Displays the coordinate of the target point used in the Dview command.
Tdcreate	Displays time and date of drawing creation. See Time.
Tdindwg	Displays total editing time. See Time.
Tdupdate	Displays time and date of last save. See Time.
Tdusrtimer	Displays user-elapsed time. See Time.
Textstyle	Displays the current text style. See Style.
Ucsname	Displays the name of the current UCS. See UCS.
Ucsorg	Displays the current UCS origin point. See UCS.
Ucsxdir	Displays the X direction of the current UCS. See UCS.
Ucsydir	Displays the Y direction of the current UCS. See UCS.

Table 6: System Variables (cont'd)

Read-only Variables	
Viewdir	Displays the view direction of the current view port. See Dview.
Viewtwist	Displays the view twist angle for the current view port. See Dview.
Vpointx	Displays the x value of the current three-dimensional viewpoint. See Vpoint.
Vpointy	Displays the y value of the current three-dimensional viewpoint. See Vpoint.
Vpointz	Displays the z value of the current three-dimensional viewpoint. See Vpoint.
Worlducs	Displays the status of the World Coordinate System. 0 = WCS is not current, 1 = WCS is current. See UCS.

Variables Accessible Only Through Setvar

You can access the following variables only through the Setvar command.

Adjustable Variables

You can alter these variables, but only through the Setvar command.

Attdia	Controls the attribute dialog box for the Insert command: 0 = no dialog box, 1 = dialog box.
Attreq	Controls the prompt for attributes. 0 = no prompt or dialog box for attributes. Attributes use default values. 1 = normal prompt or dialog box upon attribute insertion.

Table 6: System Variables (cont'd)

Adjustable Variables	
Cmdecho	Used with AutoLISP to control what is displayed on the prompt line. See the AutoLISP manual for details.
Dragp1	Controls regen-drag input sampling rate.
Dragp2	Controls fast-drag input sampling rate. Higher values force the display of more of the dragged image during cursor movement while lower values display less.
Expert	Controls prompts, depending on level of user's expertise. 0 issues normal prompts. 1 suppresses *About to Regen* and *Really want to turn the current light off?* prompts. 2 suppresses previous prompts plus *Block already defined* and *A drawing with this name already exists*. 3 suppresses previous prompts plus line type warnings. 4 suppresses previous prompts plus UCS and Vports *Save* warnings.
Flatland	Controls AutoCAD's handling of three-dimensional functions and objects as they relate to Object snaps, DXF formats, and AutoLISP. 0 = functions take advantage of version 10's advanced features, 1 = functions operate as they did prior to version 10.
Highlight	Controls object-selection ghosting: 0 = no ghosting, 1 = ghosting.
Menuecho	Controls the display of commands and prompts issued from the menu. A value of 1 suppresses display of commands entered from menu (can be toggled on or off with Ctrl-P); 2 suppresses display of commands and command prompts when command is issued from AutoLISP macro; 3 is a combination of options 1 and 2; 4 disables Ctrl-P menu echo toggle.

Table 6: System Variables (cont'd)

Adjustable Variables	
Mirrtext	Controls text mirroring: 0 = no text mirroring, 1 = text mirroring.
Pdmode	Controls the type of symbol used as a point during the Point command. Several point styles are available. See **Point**.
Pdsize	Controls the size of the symbol set by Pdmode.
Pickbox	Controls the size of the object-selection box. You can enter integer values to control the box height in pixels.
Skpoly	Controls whether the Sketch command uses regular lines or polylines. 0 = line, 1 = polyline.
Splframe	Controls the display of spline vertices, surface fit three-dimensional meshes, and invisible edges of 3dfaces. 0 = no display of Spline vertices of invisible 3dface edges. Displays only defining mesh or surface fit mesh. 1 = display of Spline vertices or invisible 3dface edges. Displays only surface fit mesh.
Splinesegs	Controls the number of line segments used for each spline patch.
Splinetype	Controls the type of curved line generated by the Pedit Spline command. 5 = quadratic B-spline, 6 = Cubic B-spline.
Surftab1	Controls the number of mesh control points for the Rulesurf and Tabsurf commands and the number of mesh points in the M direction for the Revsurf and Edgesurf commands.
Surftab2	Controls the number of mesh control points in the N direction for the Revsurf and Edgesurf commands.

Table 6: System Variables (cont'd)

Adjustable Variables	
Surftype	Controls the type of surface fitting generated by the Pedit Smooth command. 5 = quadratic B-spline, 6 = cubic B-spline, and 8 = Bezier surface.
Surfu	Controls the accuracy of the smoothed surface models in the M direction.
Surfv	Controls the accuracy of the smoothed surface models in the N direction.
Texteval	Controls whether prompts for text and attribute input to commands are taken literally or as AutoLISP expressions. 0 = literal, 1 = text you input with left parens and exclamation points will be interpreted as AutoLISP expression. Dtext takes all input literally, regardless of this setting.
Ucsfollow	Controls whether changing the current UCS automatically displays the plan view of the new current UCS. 0 = displayed view does not change, 1 = automatic display of new current UCS in plan.
Useri1-5	Five variables for storing integers for custom applications.
Userr1-5	Five variables for storing real numbers for custom applications.
Worldview	Controls whether point input to the Dview and Vpoint commands is relative to the WCS or the current UCS. 0 = commands use the current UCS to interpret point value input, 1 = commands use UCS to interpret point value input.

Table 6: System Variables (cont'd)

Read-only Variables

These read-only variables can be read only through the Setvar command, unlike the variables in the first two sections of this table.

Acadprefix	Displays the name of the directory saved in the DOS environment using the DOS command SET.
Dwgprefix	Displays drive and directory prefix for drawing file.
Extmax	Displays upper-right corner coordinate of drawing extent.
Extmin	Displays lower-left corner coordinate of drawing extent.
Screensize	Reads the size of the graphics screen in pixels.
Tempprefix	Displays the name of the directory where temporary AutoCAD files are saved.
Viewctr	Displays the center coordinate of the current view.
Viewsize	Displays the height of the current view in drawing units.
Vsmax	Displays the three-dimensional coordinate of the upper-right corner of the current viewport's virtual screen relative to the current UCS.
Vsmin	Displays the three-dimensional coordinate of the lower-left corner of the current viewport's virtual screen relative to the current UCS.

TABLES (AUTOLISP)

- **VERSIONS**   10, 11

- **PURPOSE**   Lists the layers, line types, views, blocks, styles, UCS, and viewports of a drawing. It demonstrates the Tblnext and Tblsearch functions of AutoLISP.

Sequence of Steps

- From the keyboard: **(load "<drive>:/<path>/tables")** ⌐ **Tables** ⌐

- From the screen menu: **Bonus-next-Tables**

Then complete the following step:

   Sort the entries (Y/N): Enter your selection.

- **NOTES**   From the keyboard, you have to load Tables only once per editing session. You can then use Tables at any time. It is not necessary to load Tables if you are using the menu.

See Also   AutoLISP

TABLET

- **VERSIONS**   All versions

- **PURPOSE**   Tablet is useful only if you have a digitizing tablet. Use it to set up your tablet for accurate tracing.

To Set Up a Tablet

- From the keyboard: **Tablet** ↵

- From the screen menu: **Settings-next-Tablet**

Then complete the following step:

Option (ON/OFF/CAL/CFG): Enter an option. If you do not have a digitizing tablet, you will get the message:

Your pointing device cannot be used as a tablet.

● OPTIONS

ON/OFF   Toggles the Calibrated mode on or off. When it is on, you cannot access the screen menus. The F10 function key performs the same function.

CAL   Allows you to calibrate a tablet so distances on the tablet correspond to distances in your drawing. The calibration is only for the space (Paper/Modelspace) in which it is performed.

CFG   Allows you to configure your digitizing tablet for a tablet menu like the one provided by AutoCAD.

● NOTES   The CAL or Calibrate option allows you to make a specific distance on the tablet correspond to a distance in your AutoCAD drawing. You are prompted to pick a first known point on the tablet and enter its corresponding coordinate in your AutoCAD drawing. This point should be at one end of a line of a known length; one end of a building plan wall known to be ten feet long, for example. Then you are prompted to pick a second known point on your tablet and enter its corresponding coordinate in your drawing. This second point should be the other end of the line of known length. For best results, this line should be as long as possible and should be horizontal or vertical, not diagonal. You may want to include a graphic scale in your drawing to be digitized just for the purpose of calibrating your tablet.

You may not be able to calibrate your tablet if you have configured it to have menus and a small screen pointing area. You may have to reconfigure it so that its entire surface is designated for the screen pointing area.

The CFG or Configure option allows you to control the location and format of tablet menus as well as the pointing area on your tablet. You are first prompted for the number of tablet menus you want. The AutoCAD tablet menu contains four. Then you are prompted to pick the upper-left, lower-left, and lower-right corners of the tablet menus. The AutoCAD template shows a black dot at these corners. Next, you are prompted for the number of columns and rows that each menu contains. Finally, you are asked if you want to specify the screen pointing area. This is the area on the tablet used for actual drawing. If you answer yes to this prompt, you are prompted to pick the lower-left and upper-right corners of the pointing area. Much of this process is automated for the standard AutoCAD tablet template when you use the Configure option found on the Screen's Settings-Tablet menu.

See Also   Sketch

TABLET MENU

- **VERSIONS**   All versions

- **PURPOSE**   Allows you to use a pointing device to activate commands from a digitizing tablet (see Figure 27).

To Use the Tablet Menu

Activate a command from the tablet by moving your pointing device to a box that represents the desired command and pressing the pick button. Commands you pick from the tablet menu often display a corresponding screen menu to allow you to pick the command options. The blank area at the top of the tablet menu is reserved for additional custom menu options.

- **NOTES**   See the Tablet command on how to configure the tablet menu for use with AutoCAD.

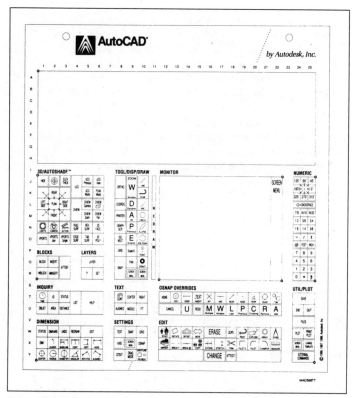

Figure 27: The AutoCAD tablet menu (Image courtesy of Autodesk Inc.)

Both the command name and an icon representing the command are displayed in boxes. These boxes are grouped into categories similar to those on the root menu.

TABSURF

- **VERSIONS**   10, 11

● **PURPOSE**   Draws a surface by extruding a curve in a straight line (see Figure 28). Before using Tabsurf, you must draw a curve defining the extruded shape and a line defining the direction of the extrusion (the direction vector).

To Draw a Curved Surface

- From the keyboard: **Tabsurf** ↵

- From the screen menu: **3D-Tabsurf** (9, 10), **Surfaces-Tabsurf** (11)

- From the pull-down menu: **Draw-Surfaces-Tabulate surface icon**

Then follow these steps:

1. **Select path curve:** Pick a curve defining the surface shape.

2. **Selecting direction vector:** Pick a line defining the direction of the extrusion.

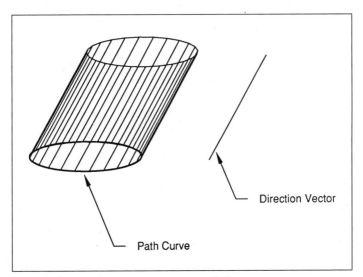

Figure 28: A curve extruded in a straight line

● **NOTES** The point at which you pick the direction vector at the **Select direction vector** prompt determines the direction of the extrusion. The end point nearest the pick point is the base of the direction vector, and the other end indicates the direction of the extrusion. You can draw the curve with a line, arc, circle, two-dimensional polyline, or three-dimensional polyline. The direction vector can be a three-dimensional line. Tabsurf has an effect similar to changing the thickness of an object, but extrusions using Tabsurf are not limited to the Z-axis.

The Surftab1 system variable will affect the number of facets used to form the surface.

See Also Command: Pedit. System Variable: Surftab1

TEDIT (DIM)

● **VERSIONS** 11

● **PURPOSE** Modifies the placement, justification, and rotation angle of associative dimension text.

Before Dimensioning

You must have issued the Dim or Dim1 command to use any dimensioning subcommand.

Sequence of Steps

- From the keyboard: **Tedit** ↵

- From the screen menu: **Dim-Tedit**

Then follow these steps:

1. **Select dimension:** Pick a single dimension.

2. **Enter text location (Left/Right/Home/Angle):** Enter an option or pick a new location for the dimension text.

You can drag the text to the next location with the cursor. If you move the text from a position in line with the dimension line, the dimension will automatically join to become a continuous line.

● OPTIONS

Left   Justifies text to the left on linear, radius, and diameter dimensions.

Right   Justifies text to the right on linear, radius, and diameter dimensions.

Home   Places text in its default dimension. This has the same effect as the Hometext subcommand.

Angle   Changes the angle for text. At the prompt Text angle, enter an angle value or indicate an angle by picking two points.

● **NOTES**   When Tedit is used on a dimension the style is updated to the current dimension style setting. If no style is associated with the dimension, then the current dimension variable settings are used.

See Also   Hometext. System Variables: Dimaso, Dimsho

TEXT

See Dtext.

TEXTSCR

See Graphscr/Textscr.

3DARRAY (AUTOLISP)

● **VERSIONS**   Version 10 and later.

● **PURPOSE**   Creates multiple copies of an object or set of objects in a three-dimensional matrix or array.

To Create a Three-Dimensional Array

- From the keyboard: **3darray** ↵
- From the pull-down menu: **Modify-3D Array** (11)

Then follow these steps:

1. **Select objects:** Select the objects to be arranged.

2. **Rectangular or Polar array (R/P):** Enter **R** for a rectangular array or **P** for a polar or circular array.

If you enter **R** at the **Rectangular or Polar** prompt, you get the following series of prompts:

3. **number of rows (---) <1>:** Enter the number of rows.

4. **number of columns (¦ ¦ ¦) <1>:** Enter the number of columns.

5. **number of levels (...) <1>:** Enter the number of levels.

If you enter **P** at the **Rectangular or Polar** prompt, you get the following prompts:

6. **Number of items:** Enter the number of items in the array, including the originally selected objects.

7. **Angle to fill <360>:** Enter the angle the array is to occupy.

8. **Rotate objects as they are copied? <Y>:** Enter **N** if the arrayed objects are to maintain their current orientation.

9. **Center point of array:** Pick the first point of the axis of rotation.

10. **Second point of axis of rotation:** Pick the other end of the axis of rotation.

See Also   Array

3DFACE

● **VERSIONS**   10

● **PURPOSE**   Allows you to draw a 3dface in three-dimensional space. 3dfaces are surfaces defined by four points in space picked in circular fashion. Though they appear transparent, 3dfaces are treated as opaque when you remove hidden lines from a drawing. After the first face is defined, you are prompted for additional third and fourth points, which allow the addition of adjoining 3dfaces.

To Draw a 3dface

- From the keyboard: **3dface** ↵

- From the screen menu: **3D-3dface** (9, 10), **Draw-next-3dface**

- From the pull-down menu: **Draw-3D Face** (11)

Then follow these steps:

1. **First point:** Select the first corner.

2. **Second point:** Select the second corner.

3. **Third point:** Select the third corner.

4. **Fourth point:** Select the fourth corner.

5. **Third point:** Continue to pick pairs of points defining more faces or press ↵ to end the command.

• OPTIONS

Enter **Invisible (I)** at the point prompt to make an edge of the 3dface invisible.

• NOTES   Use the Invisible option if you want to hide the joint line between joined 3dfaces. Enter **I** just before you pick the first defining point of the side to be made invisible.

Make invisible edges visible by setting the Splframe system variable to any nonzero value. See **Setvar** for more on Splframe.

All meshes are composed of 3dfaces. If you explode a 3dmesh, each facet of the mesh will be a 3dface.

See Also   System Variables: Pfacevmax, Splframe

3DMESH

• VERSIONS   10 and later.

• PURPOSE   Draws a three-dimensional surface using coordinate values you specify. 3dmesh can be used when drawing three-dimensional models of a topography or performing finite element analysis. 3dmesh is designed for programmers who want control over each node of a mesh.

To Draw with 3dmesh

- From the keyboard: **3dmesh** ↵

- From the screen menu: **3d-3dmesh** (9, 10), **Surfaces-3dmesh** (11)

Then follow these steps:

1. **Mesh M size:** Enter the number of vertices in the M direction.

2. **Mesh N size:** Enter the number of vertices in the N direction.

3. **Vertex (0,0):** Enter the X,Y,Z coordinate value for the first vertex in the mesh.

4. **Vertex (0,1):** Enter the X,Y,Z coordinate value for the next vertex in the N direction of the mesh.

5. **Vertex (0,2):** Continue to enter X,Y,Z coordinate values for the vertices.

● **NOTES**   To use 3dmesh to generate a topographic model, arrange your X,Y,Z coordinate values in a rectangular array, roughly as they would appear in the plan. Fill any blanks in the array with dummy or neutral coordinate values. Start the 3dmesh command and use the number of columns for the mesh M size and the number of rows for the N size. At the **Vertex** prompts, enter the coordinate values row by row, starting at the lower-left corner of your array and reading from left to right. Include any dummy values.

See Also   Commands: Mface, Pedit, Pface. System Variables: Surftype, Surfu, Surfv

3DPOLY

● **VERSIONS**   10 and later.

● **PURPOSE** Allows you to draw a polyline in three-dimensional space using X, Y, and Z coordinates or object snap points. Three-dimensional polylines are like standard polylines, except that you can't give them a width or use arc segments. Also, you cannot use the Pedit command's Fit curve option with 3dpoly. To create a smooth curve using three-dimensional polylines, use the Spline Pedit option.

To Draw a 3dpoly Line

- From the keyboard: **3dpoly** ↵

- From the screen menu: **3D-3dpoly**

- From the pull-down menu: **Draw-3D poly(line)**

Then follow these steps:

1. **From point:** Enter the beginning point.

2. **Close/Undo/<Endpoint of line>:** Enter the next point of the line.

3. **Close/Undo/<Endpoint of line>:** Continue to pick points for additional line segments or press ↵ to end the command.

● **OPTIONS**

Close Connects the first point with the last point in a series of line segments.

Undo Moves back one line segment in a series of line segments.

See Also Commands: Pedit, Pline

TIME

● **VERSIONS** 2.5 and later

● **PURPOSE**   Keeps track of the time you spend on a drawing. The time is displayed in "military" format, using the 24-hour count.

Sequence of Steps

- From the keyboard: **Time** ⏎

- From the screen menu: **Inquiry-Time**

Then complete the following step:

Current time:	*(date and time)*
Drawing created:	*(date and time)*
Drawing last updated:	*(date and time)*
Time in drawing editor:	*(days and time)*
Elapsed time:	*(days and time)*
(elapsed timer status)	
Display/On/Off/Reset: Enter an option.	

● **OPTIONS**

Display   Redisplays time information.

On   Sets elapsed timer on.

Off   Sets elapsed timer off.

Reset   Resets elapsed timer to 0.

See Also   System Variables: Tdcreate, Tdindwg, Tdupdate, Tdusrtimer

TRACE

● **VERSIONS**   All versions

● **PURPOSE**   You can use Trace where a thick line is desired. Alternatively, you can accomplish the same thing by using the Pline command. If you draw a series of Trace line segments, the corners are automatically joined to form a sharp corner.

To Draw a Thick Line

• From the keyboard: **Trace** ↵

• From the screen menu: **Draw-next-Trace**

Then follow these steps:

1. **Trace width <default width>:** Enter the desired width.

2. **From point:** Pick the start point for the trace.

3. **To point:** Pick the next point.

As with the Line command, you can continue to pick points to draw a series of connected line segments.

See Also   Command: Fill. System Variable: Tracewid

TRANSPARENT COMMANDS

● **VERSIONS**   2.6 and later

● **PURPOSE**   Transparent commands are ones which can be used while you are in the middle of another command. To use a transparent command transparently, you must, when entering the command name, precede it with an apostrophe. In version 11, all system variables can be accessed transparently by entering the variable name preceded by an apostrophe.

● **OPTIONS**

AutoCAD's transparent commands are Ddemodes, Ddlmodes, Ddrmodes, Graphscr, Help/?, Pan, Redraw, Redrawall, Resume, Setvar, Textscr, View, and Zoom.

The commands that start with *Dd* open dialog boxes that let you control entity creation and layer and drawing modes.

TRIM

● **VERSIONS**   2.5 and later. The Undo option is added in 11.

● **PURPOSE**   Trim shortens an object to meet another object.

Sequence of Steps

- From the keyboard: **Trim** ↵

- From the screen menu: **Edit-next-Trim**

- From the pull-down menu: **Edit-Trim** (9), **Modify-Trim** (10, 11)

Then follow these steps:

1. **Select cutting edge(s)**... Pick the objects to which you want to trim other objects.

2. **<Select objects to trim>/Undo:** Pick the objects you want to trim one at a time.

Versions prior to 11 display the **Select objects** prompt in step 1.

● **NOTES**   At the **Select cutting edge** prompt, you can pick several objects that intersect the objects you want to trim. Once you've selected the cutting edges, press ↵ and the **Select object** prompt appears, allowing you to pick the objects to trim. You cannot trim objects within blocks or use blocks as cutting edges. In addition, cutting edges must intersect the objects to be trimmed. If you pick an object that falls between two other "cutting edge" objects, the segment between the "cutting edge" objects will be removed.

You can only use Trim on objects that lie in a plane parallel to the current User Coordinate System. In addition, if you are not viewing the current UCS in plan, you may get an erroneous result.

See Also   Break, Change

TROTATE (DIM)

● **VERSIONS**   11

● **PURPOSE**   Changes the rotation angle of associative dimension text.

Before Dimensioning

You must have issued the Dim or Dim1 command to use any dimensioning subcommand.

Sequence of Steps

● From the keyboard: **Trotate** ⏎

Then follow these steps:

1. **Enter new text angle:** Enter the angle value or indicate the angle by picking two points.

2. **Select objects:** Pick the associative dimensions that you want to change.

● **NOTES**   If you enter a 0 for the rotation angle, the text returns to its default angle. Trotate updates the dimension to the current settings for its associated dimension style. If no style is associated with the dimension, then the current dimension variable settings are used.

See Also   Restore, Save. Dimension Variables: Dimtih, Dimtoh

TYPE

● **VERSIONS**   2.1 and later

● **PURPOSE**   Performs the same function as the DOS command, which is also called Type. It displays the contents of a DOS text file or ASCII file. If the DOS More.COM file is available, you can use the DOS command modifier ¦ **more** to display large files.

To View a Text File

- From the keyboard: **Type** ↵

- From the screen menu: **Utility-External Command-Type**

Then complete the following step:

File to list: Key in a DOS or ASCII file name.

See Also   Acad.pgp

U

● **VERSIONS**   2.5 and later

● **PURPOSE**   Reverses the most recent command. You can undo as many commands as you have issued during any given editing session. However, you cannot undo commands after a Plot or Prplot command has occurred.

To Undo a Command

- From the keyboard: **U** ↵

- From the pull-down menu: **Tools-U** (9), **Utility-U** (11)

● **NOTES**   The Auto, End, Control, and Group options under the Undo command affect the results of the U command.

See Also   Commands: Redo, Undo

UCS

● **VERSIONS**   10 and later

● **PURPOSE**   The User Coordinate System, or UCS, is a tool for creating and editing three-dimensional drawings. A UCS can be described as a plane in three-dimensional space on which you can draw. Using the UCS command, you can create and shift between as many UCS planes as you like.

There are specialized three-dimensional drawing commands for creating three-dimensional surfaces. You can issue these three-dimensional commands independently of the UCS. In general, however, objects are drawn on or parallel to the plane of a UCS.

To Modify a UCS

- From the keyboard: **UCS** ↵

- From the screen menu: **UCS-UCS**

Then complete the following step:

Origin/ZAxis/3point/Entity/View/X/Y/Z/Prev/Restore/ Save/Del/?/<World>: Enter an option.

● OPTIONS

Origin   Determines the origin of a UCS.

ZAxis   Defines the direction of the Z-coordinate axis. You are prompted for an origin for the UCS and for a point along the Z-axis of the UCS.

3point   Allows you to define a UCS by selecting three points: the origin, a point along the positive direction of the X-axis, and a point along the positive direction of the Y-axis.

Entity   Defines a UCS based on the orientation of an object.

View   Defines a UCS parallel to your current view. The origin of the current UCS will be used as the origin of the new UCS.

X/Y/Z   Allows you to define a UCS by rotating the current UCS about its X-, Y-, or Z-axis.

Prev   Places you in the previously defined UCS. The UCS Previous option under the Settings pull-down menu has the same effect.

Restore   Restores a saved UCS.

Save   Saves a UCS for later recall.

Del   Deletes a previously saved UCS.

?   Displays a list of currently saved UCSs. You can use wildcard filter lists to search for specific UCS names.

World   Returns you to the World Coordinate System.

● **NOTES**   The World Coordinate System, or WCS, is the base from which all other UCSs are defined. The WCS is the default coordinate system when you open a new file.

When you pick UCS options from the Settings pull-down menu, an icon menu appears that contains several predefined UCS options. When you pick an option, you are prompted for an origin. This allows you either to accurately place the plane by selecting a point on an existing three-dimensional object or to specify numerical coordinates for the UCS origin.

If you use the Entities option, the way the selected entity was created affects the orientation of the UCS. Table 7 correlates selected entities with UCS orientation.

See Also   Commands: Dducs, Dview, Elev, Plan, Rename, Thickness, Ucsicon, Vpoint, Wildcards. System Variables: Ucsfollow, Ucsicon, Ucsname, Ucsorg, Ucsxdir, Ucsydir, Worlducs, Vsmax, Vsmin

UCSICON

● **VERSIONS**   10

● **PURPOSE**   Controls the display and location of the UCS icon. The UCS icon tells you the orientation of the current UCS. It displays an "L" shaped graphic showing the positive X and Y directions. When the WCS is the current default coordinate system the icon displays a W. If the current UCS plane is perpendicular to your current view, the UCS icon displays a broken pencil to indicate that you will have difficulty drawing in the current view. The UCS icon changes to a cube when you are displaying a perspective view. When you are in Paperspace, it turns into a triangle.

To Modify the UCS Icon

●   From the keyboard: **Ucsicon** ↵

Then complete the following step:

ON/OFF/All/Noorigin/ORigin <ON>: Enter an option.

Table 7: UCS Generation Based on Entities

Object Type	UCS Orientation
Arc	The center of the arc establishes the UCS origin. The X-axis of the UCS passes through the pick point on the arc.
Circle	The center of the circle establishes the UCS origin. The X-axis of the UCS passes through the pick point on the circle.
Dimension	The midpoint of the dimension text establishes the UCS origin. The X-axis of the UCS is parallel to the X-axis that was active when the dimension was drawn.
Line	The end point nearest the pick point establishes the origin of the UCS, and the XZ plane of the UCS contains the line.
Point	The point location establishes the UCS origin. The UCS orientation is arbitrary.
2D Polyline	The starting point of the polyline establishes the UCS origin. The X-axis is determined by the direction from the first point to the next vertex.
Solid	The first point of the solid establishes the origin of the UCS. The second point of the solid establishes the X-axis.
Trace	The direction of the trace establishes the X-axis of the UCS with the beginning point setting the origin.
3Dface	The first point of the 3Dface establishes the origin. The first and second points establish the X-axis. The plane defined by the face determines the orientation of the UCS.
Shapes, Text, Blocks, Attributes, and Attribute Definitions	The insertion point establishes the origin of the UCS. The object's rotation angle establishes the X-axis.

● OPTIONS

ON   Turns the UCS icon on.

OFF   Turns the UCS icon off.

All   Forces the Ucsicon settings to take effect in all viewports if you have more than one viewport. Otherwise, the settings will only affect the active view port.

Noorigin   Places the UCS icon in the lower-left corner of the drawing area, regardless of the current UCS's origin location.

ORigin   Places the UCS icon at the origin of the current UCS. If the origin is off the screen, the UCS icon will appear in the lower-left corner of the drawing area.

See Also   Commands: UCS, Viewports. System Variable: Ucsicon

UNDEFINE

See Redefine.

UNDO

● VERSIONS   2.5 and later

● PURPOSE   Allows you to undo parts of your editing session. This can be useful if you accidentally execute a command that destroys part or all of your drawing. Undo also allows you to control how much of a drawing is undone.

To Undo Edits

- From the keyboard: **Undo** ↵

- From the screen menu: **Edit-next-Undo**

- From the pull-down menu: **Utility-Undo Mark or Undo Back** (see Mark and Back options) (11)

Then complete the following step:

Auto/Back/Control/End/Group/Mark/<default number>:
Enter an option to use or the number of commands to undo.

● OPTIONS

Auto   Makes AutoCAD view menu macros as a single command. If Auto is set to On, the effect of macros issued from a menu will be undone regardless of the number of commands the macro contains.

Back, Mark   Allow you to experiment safely with a drawing by first marking a point in your editing session to which you can return. Once a mark has been issued, you can proceed with your experimental drawing addition. Then, you can use Back to undo all the commands back to the place that Mark was issued.

End, Group   Allow you to mark a group of commands to be undone together. Issue the Undo/Group command and proceed with your editing until you reach the point where you wish to end the group. Then, issue the Undo/End command. If you use the U command, the commands issued between the Undo/Group and the Undo/End commands will be treated as a single command and will all be undone at once.

Control   Allows you to turn off the Undo feature to save disk space or to limit the Undo feature to single commands. You are prompted for All, None, or One. All fully enables the Undo feature, None disables Undo, and One restricts the Undo feature to a single command at a time.

● NOTES
Many commands offer an Undo option. The Undo option under a main command will act more like the U command and will not offer the options described here.

See Also   Commands: Redo, U

UNDO (DIM)

● **VERSIONS**   2.5 and later

● **PURPOSE**   Rescinds a dimension you decide you do not want, as long as you remain in the dimension mode. If you issue Undo during the Leader command, the last leader line segment drawn will be undone.

Before Dimensioning

You must have issued the Dim or Dim1 command to use any dimensioning subcommand.

To Undo a Dimension

- From the keyboard: **Undo** ⏎

- From the screen menu: **Dim-Undo**

● **NOTES**   You can enter **U** in place of **Undo**.

UNITS

● **VERSIONS**   All versions (some options added later)

● **PURPOSE**   Sets AutoCAD to the unit format appropriate to the drawing. For example, if you are drawing an architectural floor plan, you can set up AutoCAD to accept and display distances using feet, inches, and fractional inches. You can also set up AutoCAD to accept and display angles as degrees, minutes, and seconds of arc rather than the default decimal degrees.

To Change Drawing Units

- From the keyboard: **Units** ⏎

- From the screen menu: **Settings-next-Units**

Then follow these steps:

1. With the exception of the Engineering and Architectural modes, you can use the modes listed below with any basic unit of measurement. For example, Decimal mode is perfect for metric units as well as decimal English units.

Report formats:	(Examples)
1. Scientific	1.55E+01
2. Decimal	15.50
3. Engineering	1'–3.50"
4. Architectural	1'–3 1/2"
5. Fractional	15 1/2

    Enter choice, 1 to 5 <2>: Enter the number corresponding to the desired unit system.

2. **Number of digits to right of decimal point (0 to 8): <4>:** Enter a number.

3. The following listing appears:

Systems of angle measure:	(Examples)
1. Decimal degrees	45.0000
2. Degrees/ minutes/seconds	45d0'0"
3. Grads	50.0000g
4. Radians	0.7854r
5. Surveyor's units	N 45d0'0" E

Enter choice, 1 to 5 <1>: Enter the number corresponding to the desired angle measure system.

4. **Number of fractional places for display of angle
   (0 to 8) <0>:** Enter a number.

5. The following listing appears:

   Direction for angle 0:
   East   3 o'clock = 0
   North 12 o'clock = 90
   West   9 o'clock = 180
   South 6 o'clock = 270

   Enter direction for angle 0 <0>: Enter the desired angle
   for the 0 degree direction.

6. **Do you want angle measured clockwise <N>:** Enter **Y**
   if you want angles measured clockwise, otherwise press ⏎.

• OPTIONS

System of units   Sets format of units that AutoCAD will accept
as input.

System of angle measure   Sets format of angle measurement
AutoCAD will accept as input.

Direction for angle 0   Sets direction for the 0 angle.

• NOTES   In versions 9 and 10, the Setup option on the root
menu automatically adjusts the Units settings based on the options
you select. Version 11 uses the VMsetup utility found on the Bonus-
next menu. If you do not like the default settings created by Setup,
you can use Units to fine-tune your settings.

Version 11 allows decimal or fractional input regardless of the unit
format being used. This means you can enter 5.5', as well as 5'6",
when using the Architectural format.

See Also   System Variables: Aflags, Angbase, Angdir, Luprec,
Unitmode

UPDATE (DIM)

• **VERSIONS**   2.6 and later

• **PURPOSE**   Changes old dimensions to new Dimension variable settings. Update only works on associative dimensions that have not been exploded.

Before Dimensioning

You must have issued the Dim or Dim1 command to use any dimensioning subcommand.

To Use Update

- From the keyboard: **Update** ↵

- From the screen menu: **Dim-next-Update**

Then complete the following step:

Select objects: Pick the associative dimensions to be updated.

See Also   Associative dimensions, Dimaso

VARIABLES (DIM)

• **VERSIONS**   11

• **PURPOSE**   Lists the dimension variable settings of a dimension style.

Before Dimensioning

You must have issued the Dim or Dim1 command before using any dimensioning subcommand.

Sequence of Steps

- From the keyboard: **Var** ↵
- From the screen menu: **Dim-next-Variables**

Then follow these steps:

1. **Current dimension style: <current style name> ?/Enter dimension style name or RETURN to select dimension:** Enter ? to view available dimension styles, enter the name of a known dimension style, or press ↵ to pick a dimension whose dimension style you wish to list. If you enter ?, you see the following prompt:

2. **Dimension style(s) to list <*>:** Enter the name specification. Wildcard characters are accepted.

After listing the dimension style names, AutoCAD returns to the prompt shown in step 1, allowing you to enter the name of a dimension style.

● **NOTES** To find the differences between the current dimension style and another style, enter a dimension style name preceded with a tilde (~) at the prompt shown in step 2. Differences are displayed in a list of dimension variable settings for each style.

See Also Restore, Save

VERTICAL (DIM)

● **VERSIONS** 1.4 and later

• **PURPOSE**   Forces a dimension to be displayed vertically, regardless of where the extension line origins are placed.

Before Dimensioning

You must have issued the Dim or Dim1 command to use any dimensioning subcommand.

Sequence of Steps

- From the keyboard: **Vertical** ↵

- From the screen menu: **Dim-Linear-Vertical**

Then follow these steps:

1. **First extension line origin or RETURN to select:** Pick one end of the object to be dimensioned.

2. **Second extension line origin:** Pick the other end of the object.

3. **Dimension line location:** Pick a point or enter a coordinate indicating the location of the dimension line.

4. **Dimension text: <default dimension>:** Press ↵ to accept the default dimensions or enter a dimension value.

The dimension text appears in the current text style.

You can issue this subcommand by entering **Ver** instead of the full word **Vertical** at the **Dim** prompt.

VIEW

• **VERSIONS**   2.0 and later

• **PURPOSE**   Allows you to save views of your drawing. Instead of using the Zoom command to zoom in and out of your drawing, you can save views of the areas you need to edit, and then recall them using the Restore option of the View command. When you key in an apostrophe followed by the command, View becomes a transparent command that can be used in the middle of another command.

To Save Views of Your Drawing

• From the keyboard: **'View.**⏎

• From the screen menu: **Display-View**

Then complete the following step:

?/Delete/Restore/Save/Window: Enter the capitalized letter of the desired option or pick an option from the menu.

● OPTIONS

? Lists all currently saved views. Wildcard filter lists are accepted.

Delete Prompts you for a view name to delete from the drawing database.

Restore Prompts you for a view name to restore to the screen.

Save Saves current view. You are prompted for a view name.

Window Saves a view defined by a window. You are prompted first to enter a view name and then to window the area to be saved as a view.

● **NOTES** To use View most effectively, keep the saved views within AutoCAD's virtual screen so that they can be restored at redraw speeds. Otherwise, restoring views may cause regeneration, which can slow down your editing. In versions 10 or earlier, use View to save an overall view of your drawing. Issuing a Zoom/All always causes a regeneration, but as long as a saved view is within the bounds of the virtual screen, restoring it requires only a redraw. In version 11, use Zoom/Vmax to get an overall view of your drawing without causing a regen.

View will save three-dimensional orthographic projection views, perspective views, and, in version 11, Paperspace or Modelspace views. View does not save hidden line views or shaded views.

See Also   Commands: Regen, Regenauto, Viewres

VIEWPORTS

See Vports.

VIEWRES

- **VERSIONS**   2.5 and later

- **PURPOSE**   Controls whether AutoCAD's virtual screen feature is used, and how accurately AutoCAD displays lines, arcs, and circles.

Sequence of Steps

- From the keyboard: **Viewres** ↵

- From the screen menu: **Display-Viewres**

Then follow these steps:

1. **Do you want fast zooms? <Y>** Enter **Y** or **N**. If you respond with Y, the following prompt appears:

2. **Enter circle zoom percent (1-20000) <current setting>:** Enter a value from 1 to 20,000 or press ↵ to accept the default.

• OPTIONS

Yes   Sets up a large virtual screen, equivalent to about 32,000 pixels square. Within this virtual screen, zooms, pans, and view/restores occur at redraw speeds. You are prompted for a circle zoom percent. This value determines how accurately circles and noncontinuous lines are shown.

No   Turns off the virtual screen. All zooms, pans, and view/restores will cause a regeneration.

• **NOTES**   The circle zoom percent value also affects the speed of redraws and regenerations. A high value slows down redraws and regenerations; a low value speeds them up. Differences in redraw speeds are barely noticeable unless you have a very large drawing.

The default value for the circle zoom percent is 100, but at this value dashed or hidden lines can appear continuous, depending on the Ltscale setting. A value of 2000 or higher reduces or eliminates this problem with little sacrifice of speed.

Use a high percent value for circle zoom to display smooth circles and arcs and to accurately show noncontinuous lines. A low value causes arcs and circles to appear as a series of line segments when viewed up close. Noncontinuous lines, however, may appear continuous. This does not mean that prints or plots of your drawing will be less accurate; only the display is affected.

A low circle zoom value causes object end points, intersections, and tangents to appear inaccurately placed when you edit a closeup view of circles and arcs. Often, this results from the segmented appearance of arcs and circles and does not necessarily mean the object placement is inaccurate. It may also be hard to distinguish between polygons and circles. Setting the circle zoom percent to a high value also reduces or eliminates these problems.

The drawing limits affect redraw speed when the virtual screen feature is turned on. If the limits are set to an area much greater than the actual drawing, redraws are slowed down.

To force the virtual screen to contain a specific area, set your limits to the area you want, set the limit's checking feature to On, and issue a Zoom/All command. The virtual screen will conform to these limits until another Regen is issued or until you pan or zoom outside of the area set by the limits.

See Also   Commands: Limits, Redraw, Regen, Regenauto

VPLAYER

● **VERSIONS**   11

● **PURPOSE**   Controls the visibility of layers for each individual viewport and allows display of different types of information in each viewport, even though the views are of the same drawing. You can use Vplayer in conjunction with overlapped viewports to create clipped views.

Sequence of Steps

● From the keyboard: **Vplayer** ⏎

Then complete the following step:

?/Freeze/Thaw/Reset/Newfrz/Vpvisdflt: Enter the desired option.

● **OPTIONS**

?   Displays the names of layers that are frozen in a given viewport. You are prompted to select a viewport. If you are in Modelspace, AutoCAD temporarily switches to Paperspace during your selection.

Freeze   Lets you specify the name of layers you want to freeze in selected viewports. You are first prompted for the names of the layers you wish to freeze, then for the viewport(s) in which to freeze them.

Thaw   Thaws layers in specific viewports. You are prompted for the layer names to thaw, then the viewports in which the layers are to be thawed.

Reset   Restores the default visibility setting for layers in a given viewport. See the Vpvisdflt option for information on default visibility.

Newfrz   Creates a new layer that is automatically frozen. You can then turn this new layer on individually for each viewport. The option Vp Frz under the Ddlmodes dialog box performs the same function.

Vpvisdflt   Presets the visibility of layers for new viewports created using Mview.

● **NOTES**   All options that prompt you for layer names allow use of wildcard characters to select multiple layer names. You can also use comma delimiters for lists of layers with dissimilar names.

See Also   Commands: DDlmodes, Layers, Mview, Mvsetup, Pspace

VPOINT

● **VERSIONS**   2.1 and later. The Rotate option was introduced with version 9.

● **PURPOSE**   Selects an orthographic, three-dimensional view of your drawing.

Sequence of Steps

● From the keyboard: **Vpoint** ↵

- From the screen menu: **Display-Vpoint**

- From the pull-down menu: **Display-3D view** (9), **Display-Vpoint 3D** (10, 11)

Then complete the following step:

Rotate/<View point> <current setting>: Enter a coordinate value, enter **R** for the Rotate option, or press ↵ to set the view with the compass and axes tripod.

● OPTIONS

Rotate   Allows you to specify a view in terms of angles from the XY plane and from the X-axis. You are prompted to **enter angle in X-Y plane from X axis**. Next, you are prompted to **enter angle from X-Y plane**.

View point   Allows you to specify your view point location by entering an X,Y,Z coordinate value.

↵   Allows you to visually select a view by pressing ↵ at the **Vpoint** prompt. You will get the compass and axes tripod.

Icon menu   If you pick 3DView or Vpoint 3D from the pull-down menu, an icon menu appears, offering several preset three-dimensional views. You can pick one of these options.

● NOTES   There are three methods for selecting a view:

- Enter a value in X, Y, and Z coordinates that represents your view point. For example, entering 1,1,–1 will give you the same view as entering 4,4,–4.

- Use the Rotate option to specify a view point as horizontal and vertical angles in relation to the last point selected. Use the ID command to establish the view target point (the last point selected) before you start Vpoint (see Figure 29).

- Press ↵ at the **Vpoint** prompt, and visually select a view point using the compass and axes tripod. To select a view, move your pointing device until the tripod indicates the desired X-, Y-, and Z-axis orientation. A cross on the compass

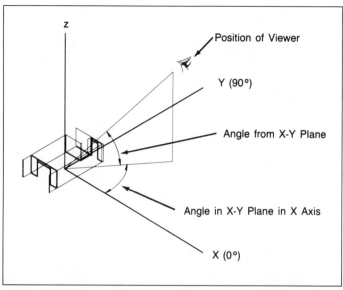

Figure 29: The viewpoint angles and what they represent

indicates your location in plan. For example, placing the cross in the lower-left quadrant of the compass places your view point below and to the left of your drawing. Your view elevation is indicated by the distance of the cross from the compass center. The closer to the center the cross is, the higher the elevation. The circle inside the compass indicates a 0 elevation. If the cross falls outside of this circle, your view elevation becomes a minus value and your view will be from below your drawing (see Figure 30).

See Also   Command: Dview

VPORTS/VIEWPORTS

● **VERSIONS**   10, 11

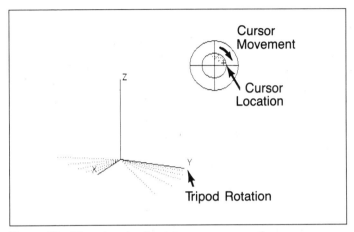

Figure 30: How the tripod rotates as you move the cursor around the target's center

● **PURPOSE** Displays multiple views, or viewports, of your drawing at once. In version 11, this command is disabled when the Tilemode system variable is set to 0. Paperspace and the Mview command then take the place of the Vports functions.

To Display Multiple Viewports

* From the keyboard: **Vports** ↵ or **Viewports** ↵

* From the screen menu: **Settings-Vports**

* From the pull-down menu: **Display-Set Viewports** (10)

Then complete the following step:

Save/Restore/Delete/Join/Single/?/2/<3>/4: Enter the desired option.

● **OPTIONS**

Save   Saves the current viewport arrangement.

Restore   Restores a previously saved viewport arrangement.

Delete   Deletes a previously saved viewport arrangement.

Join   Joins two adjacent viewports of the same size to make one larger viewport.

Single   Changes the display to a single viewport.

?   Displays a list of saved viewport arrangements along with each viewport's coordinate location.

2   Splits the display to show two viewports. You are prompted for a horizontal or vertical split.

3   Changes the display to show three viewports.

4   Changes the display to show four equal viewports.

● **NOTES**   Each viewport can contain any type of view you like. For example, you can display a perspective view in one viewport and a plan view of the same drawing in another viewport.

You can only work in one viewport at a time. To change active viewports, pick any point inside the desired viewport. The border around the selected viewport will thicken to show that it is active. The standard cursor appears only in the active viewport. When you move the cursor into an inactive viewport, it changes into an arrow. Any edits made in one viewport are immediately reflected in the other viewports.

Each viewport has its own virtual display within which you can pan and zoom at redraw speeds. For this reason, the Regen and Redraw commands affect only the active viewport. To regenerate or redraw all the viewports at once, use the Regenall and Redrawall commands.

You can pick from several predefined viewport arrangements by selecting the one you want from an icon menu. You can access the Viewports icon menu by picking the Set Viewports option on the Display pull-down menu.

See Also Commands: Mview Redraw, Redrawall, Regen, Regenall, Viewres. System Variables: Cvports, Maxactvp, Viewdir, Viewtwist, Vsmax, Vsmin

VSLIDE

● **VERSIONS** All versions

● **PURPOSE** Displays Slide files. For versions up to 2.6, slides are always individual files with the extension .SLD. Version 9 and 10 offer a slide library facility that combines a set of slides into one file. Slide library files have .SLB extensions. To view a slide from a slide library, enter the slide library name followed by the slide's name in parentheses, as in **library(slide)**.

To Display Slide Files

- From the keyboard: **Vslide** ↵

- From the screen menu: **Utility-Slides-Vslide**

Version 11 displays a files dialog box. Earlier versions display the following prompt:

File name <current file name>: Enter the name of the slide file to be displayed.

See Also Commands: Mslide, Slidelib.EXE

WBLOCK

● **VERSIONS** All versions

● **PURPOSE**   Lets you create a new file from a portion of the current file or from a block of the current file.

Sequence of Steps

- From the keyboard: **Wblock** ⏎

- From the screen menu: **Blocks-Wblock**

Then follow these steps:

Version 11 displays a files dialog box. Earlier versions display the prompt in step 1:

1. **File name:** Enter the filename

2. **Block name:** Enter the block name or press ⏎ to select objects. The block or set of objects will be written to your disk as a drawing file.

● **NOTES**   If you are exporting a block and you want the file name to be the same as the block name, enter an equal sign at the **Block name** prompt.

If you enter the name of an existing file at the **File name** prompt, you receive the prompt:

**A drawing with this name already exists.
Do you want to replace it? <N>**

You can replace the file or return to the **Command** prompt to re-start Wblock.

To write a portion of the current drawing view to a file, press ⏎ without entering anything at the **Block name** prompt. You receive the following two prompts:

Insertion base point: Enter a coordinate or pick a point.

Select objects: Select objects using the standard AutoCAD selection options.

The objects you select are written to your disk as a drawing file. The point you select at the **Insertion base point** prompt becomes the origin of the written file. The current UCS becomes the WCS in the written file. When you save a block to disk, the UCS active at the time you create the block becomes the WCS of the written file.

Entering an asterisk (*) at the **Block name** prompt writes the entire current file to disk, stripping it of all unused blocks, layers, line types, and text styles. This can reduce a file's size and access time.

Objects are placed in the Modelspace of the output file unless the asterisk is used. If the asterisk is used objects are placed in the space they are in.

See Also   Commands: Base, Files dialog box, Object selection

WILDCARD CHARACTERS

● **VERSIONS**   All versions. Version 11 has an extended set of wildcard characters.

● **PURPOSE**   Wildcard characters allow you to specify names whenever you are using a command that produces a list of names. These characters are extensions of the standard DOS wildcard characters.

To Create Lists of Names

At any prompt that asks for names to list, enter a name containing wildcard characters.

● OPTIONS

Matches any number (11). For example, **C#D** selects all names that begin with C, end with D, and have a single digit number between.

@   Matches any alphabetical character (11). For example, **C@D** selects any name that begins with C, ends with D, and has an alphabetical character between.

. (period)   Matches any character not numeric or alphabetical (11). For example, **C.D** might select the name C+D.

* (asterisk)   Matches any string of characters (all versions). For example, ***CD** selects all names that end with CD.

? (question mark)   Matches any single character (all versions). For example **C?D** selects all names of three characters that begin with C and end with D.

~ (tilde)   Matches anything but the set of characters that follow (11). For example, **~CD** selects all names that do not include CD.

[*characters*]   Matches any one of the characters enclosed in brackets (11). For example, **[CD]X** selects the names CX and DX but not CDX.

- (hyphen)   Lets you specify a range of characters when used within brackets (11). For example, **[C-F]X** selects the names CX, DX, EX, and FX.

\ (reverse quote)   Forces the character that follows to be read literally (11). For example, ***CD** selects the name *CD, instead of all names that end in CD.

● **NOTES**   Brackets can be used in conjunction with other wildcard characters. For example, you could use **[~CD]X** to find all names except CX and DX.

XBIND

● **VERSIONS**   11

● **PURPOSE**   Imports a block, dimension style, layer, line type, or text style from a cross-referenced file.

Sequence of Steps

- From the keyboard: **Xbind** ↵

- From the screen menu: **Blocks-Xbind**

Then follow these steps:

1. **Block/Dimstyle/LAyer/LType/Style:** Enter the desired option.

2. You are then prompted for the name of the item to import. Enter a single name, a list of names separated by commas, or use wildcard characters to specify a range of names.

● **NOTES**   Named variables from a cross-referenced file are prefixed with their source file name. For example, a block named Wheel from a cross-referenced file called Car will have the name Car|wheel in the file that has the cross-reference assigned to it. When you use Xbind to import the Wheel block, its name will change to Car0wheel to reflect its source file. If a block Car0wheel already exists, the 0 is replaced with a 1 as in Car1wheel.

See Also   Command: Xref

XDATA/
XDLIST (AUTOLISP)

● **VERSIONS**   11

● **PURPOSE**   Xdata lets you attach extended entity data to an object. This data can be accessed through an ADS or Autolisp application.

Sequence of Steps

- From the keyboard: **(load "<drive>:/<path>/xdata").⏎ xdata.⏎**

- From the screen menu: **Bonus-next-Xdata**

Then follow these steps:

1. **Select object:** Pick a single entity.

2. **Application name:** Enter the name of an application. If there is no application, enter any name you like. The application name is attached to the object with the group code 1001.

3. **3Real/DIR/DISP/DIST/Hdnd/Int/LAyer/LOng/Pos Real/SCale/STr/<Exit>:** Enter the desired option.

● **OPTIONS**

3Real   Attaches a list of 3 reals (as in coordinates) with the group code of 1010.

DIR   Attaches a direction value with a group code of 1013.

DISP)   Attaches a displacement value with a group code of 1012.

DIST   Attaches a distance value with a group code of 1042.

Hand   Attaches an entity handle with a group code 1005.

Int   Attaches an integer (16 bit) with a group code 1070.

LAyer   Attaches a layer name with a group code 1003.

LOng   Attaches an integer (32 bit) with a group code 1071.

Pos   Attaches a 3D world space position with a group code 1011.

Real   Attaches a real number with a group code of 1040.

SCale   Attaches a scale factor with the group code 1042.

STr   Attaches a string with a group code of 1000.

<Exit>   Exits Xdata and attaches the data to the selected object.

● **NOTES**   Group codes are integer codes used to identify properties of an object. They are used mainly with AutoLISP and in the AutoCAD DXF file format.

You can use the Xdlist AutoLISP utility to get a listing of data stored with Xdata. Xdlist is automatically loaded with Xdata so that once you load Xdata you can enter Xdlist. You are prompted to pick an object, then the application name.

From the keyboard, you have to load Xdata only once per editing session. You can then use Xdata at any time. It is not necessary to load Xdata if you are using the menu.

XPLODE (AUTOLISP)

● **VERSIONS**   11 (version 10 offers Lxplode, a similar but limited version of Xplode)

● **PURPOSE**   Xplode lets you explode multiple objects as well as control their color, layer, and line type.

Sequence of Steps

- From the keyboard: **(load "<drive>:/<path>/xplode")**↵**xp**↵

- From the screen menu: **Bonus-next-Xplode**

Then follow these steps:

1. **Select entities to Xplode**
   Select objects: Select the objects you want to explode.

2. ***n* entities found. *n* invalid.**
   Xplode Individually/<Globally>: Enter the desired option. Once you enter an option, you get the following prompt:

3. **All/Color/LAyer/LType/Inherit from parent block/ <Explode>**: Enter the desired option.

If you selected Individually in step 2, the prompt in step 3 appears for each valid selected object. If you selected Globally the prompt in step 3 appears only once.

● OPTIONS

Individually/<Globally>   Allows you to apply the other options to each selected object individually or all at once.

All   Sets the color, layer, and line type of the exploded entities.

Color   Sets only the color of the exploded entities.

LAyer   Sets only the layer of the exploded entities.

LType   Sets only the line type of the exploded entities.

Inherit from parent block   Causes the exploded entities to take on the properties of the original block.

<Explode>   Explodes the selected entities just as would the standard Explode command.

● NOTES
From the keyboard, you have to load Xplode only once per editing session. You can then use Xplode at any time. It is not necessary to load Xplode if you are using the menu.

See Also   Command: Explode

XREF

● **VERSIONS**   11

● **PURPOSE**   Xref lets you attach an external file to your current file for reference purposes.

Sequence of Steps

- From the keyboard: **Xref** ↵
- From the screen menu: **Blocks-Xref**
- From the pull-down menu: **Draw-Xref**

Then complete the following step:

> **?/Bind/Detach/Path/Reload/<Attach>:** Enter the desired option.

● **OPTIONS**

?   Displays a list of cross-referenced files in your current drawing. The name of the file as well as its location on your storage device is shown. You can filter the Xrefed file names by using wildcard characters.

Bind   Causes a cross-referenced file to become a part of the current file. Once Bind is used, the cross-referenced file becomes an ordinary block in the current file. You are prompted for the name of the Xrefed file to be bound.

Detach   Detaches a cross-referenced file, so it is no longer referenced to the current file.

Path   Lets you specify a new DOS path for a cross-referenced file. This is useful if you have moved an Xrefed file to another drive or directory. You are prompted for the Xref's name, its old path and its new path.

Reload   Lets you reload a cross reference without exiting and re-entering the current file. This option is useful if you are in a network environment and you know that someone has just finished updating a file you are using as a cross-reference.

Attach   Lets you attach another drawing file as a cross-reference. You are prompted for a file name.

● **NOTES**   Xrefed files act like blocks; they cannot be edited from the file they are attached to. The difference between blocks and Xrefed files is that Xrefed files do not become part of the current files database. Instead, the current file "points" to the Xrefed file. The next time the current file is opened, the Xrefed file is also opened and automatically attached. This has two advantages. Firstly, since the Xrefed file does not become part of the current file, the current file size remains small. Secondly, since the Xrefed file stays independent, any changes made to it are automatically reflected in the current file whenever it is re-opened.

In most of the options, you can enter a single name, a list of names separated by commas, or a name containing wildcard characters.

Named variables from the Xrefed files will have the file name as a prefix. For example, a layer called *wall* in an Xrefed file called *house* will have the name House | wall in the current file.

At the file name prompt, you can assign a name to an Xrefed file that is different from its actual file name by following the file name with an equal sign and the new name. For example:

newplan=oldplan

where newplan is the new name and oldplan is the file name of the Xrefed file.

Use the tilde (~) at the file name prompt to request a files dialog box. This dialog box can help you locate files.

AutoCAD keeps a log of Xref activity in an ASCII file. This file has the same root name as your current drawing file and has the extension .XLG. You can delete this file with no effect on your drawing.

See Also   Commands: Block, Files Dialog Box, Insert, Xbind

XREFCLIP (AUTOLISP)

- **VERSIONS**   11

- **PURPOSE**   Xrefclip lets you add an Xref file to the current drawing and "clip" the Xref's display.

Sequence of Steps

- From the keyboard: **(load "<drive>:/<path>/xrefclip").⏎ XC⏎**

- From the screen menu: **Bonus-next-Xrefclip**

If tilemode is set to 1, you get the following prompt:

1. **Paperspace/Modelspace is disabled. This routine will not run unless it is enabled. Enable Paper/ Modelspace?<Y>:** Enter **Y** to enable Paperspace. A message appears telling you that you are entering Paperspace and to use the Mview command to create viewports. Then, the next prompt appears:

2. **Xref name:** Enter the name of the file to be cross-referenced.

3. **XrefClip onto what layer:** Enter the name of a new layer.

The Xref file appears and fills the current view. The next pair of prompts asks you to locate the area you want clipped:

4. **First point of clip box:** Pick a point locating one corner of the clip rectangle.

5.   **Other point of clip box:** Pick the opposite corner of the clip rectangle.

The Xref is clipped to the rectangle and you are next prompted for the scale of the clipped Xref and its location.

6.   **Enter the ratio of paper space units to model space units...**
Number of paper space units. <1.0>: Enter a value.

7.   **Number of model space units. <1.0>:** Enter a value.

8.   **Insertion point for XrefClip:** Pick a point to locate the XrefClip viewport.

● **NOTES**   From the keyboard, it is necessary to load Xrefclip only once per editing session. You can then use Xrefclip at any time. It is not necessary to load Xrefclip if you are using the menu.

See Also   Commands: Mview, Mvsetup, Xref, Zoom/XP. System Variable: Tilemode

ZOOM

● **VERSIONS**   All versions. The XP and Vmax options are new in version 11. The Dynamic option was introduced with version 2.5. The Previous option was introduced with version 2.1.

● **PURPOSE**   Zoom controls the display of your drawing. Zoom can be used transparently when issued from the menu system or when an apostrophe is entered in front of the command.

Sequence of Steps

• From the keyboard: **'Zoom** ↵

• From the screen menu: **Display-Zoom**

- From the pull-down menu: **Display-Window**, **Previous**, **Dynamic** (9), **Display-Zoom**… (10, 11)

Then complete the following step:

**All/Center/Dynamic/Extents/Left/Previous
Vmax/Window/
<Scale(X/XP)>:** Enter the desired option.

● OPTIONS

All   Displays the area of the drawing defined by its limits or extents, whichever are greater (see Limits).

Center   Displays a view based on a selected point. You are first prompted for a center point for your view and then for a magnification or height. A value followed by an X is read as a magnification factor; a lone value is read as the desired height in drawing units of the display.

Dynamic   Displays the virtual screen and allows you to use a view box to select a view. The drawing extents, current view, and the current virtual screen area are indicated as a solid white box, a dotted green box, and red corner marks, respectively. You can pan, enlarge, or shrink the view by moving the view box to a new location, adjusting its size, or both. Whenever the view box moves into an area that will cause a regeneration, an hourglass appears in the lower-left corner of the display (see Figure 31).

Extents   Displays a view of the entire drawing. The drawing is forced to fit within the display and is forced to the left. The drawing limits (see **Limits**) are ignored.

Left   Similar to the Center option, but the point you pick at the prompt becomes the lower-left corner of the display.

Previous   Displays the last view created by a Zoom, Pan, or View command. AutoCAD will store up to four previous views (ten views for version 10).

Vmax   Displays an overall view of the current virtual display. Unlike the Extents and All options, no regen occurs.

Window   Enlarges a rectangular area of a drawing, based on a defined window.

Scale(X)   Expands or shrinks the drawing display. If an X follows the scale factor, it will be in relation to the current view. If no X is used, the scale factor will be in relation to the area defined by the limits of the drawing.

Scale(XP)   Sets a viewports scale in relation to the Paperspace scale. For example, if you have set up a title block in Paperspace at a scale of 1" = 1", and your full scale Modelspace drawing is to be at a final plot scale of 1/4" = 1', you can enter **1/48xp** at the Zoom prompt to set the viewport at the appropriate scale for Paperspace. You must be in Modelspace to use this option.

● **NOTES**   Zoom is a transparent command, which means you can use it in the middle of another command by preceding it with an apostrophe. You cannot, however, use it while viewing a drawing in perspective. Use the Dview command's Zoom option instead.

See Also   Commands: Limits, Mspace, Mview, Mvsetup, Pspace, Redraw, Regen, Regenauto, Viewres. System Variable: Viewsize

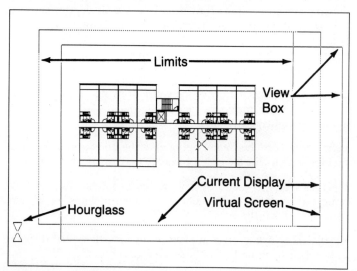

Figure 31: The Dynamic Zoom display

Index

Selections from The SYBEX Library

CAD

The ABC's of AutoCAD (Second Edition)
Alan R. Miller
375pp. Ref. 584-0

This brief but effective introduction to AutoCAD quickly gets users drafting and designing with this complex CADD package. The essential operations and capabilities of AutoCAD are neatly detailed, using a proven, step-by-step method that is tailored to the results-oriented beginner.

The ABC's of AutoLISP
George Omura
300pp. Ref. 620-0

This book is for users who want to unleash the full power of AutoCAD through the AutoLISP programming language. In non-technical terms, the reader is shown how to store point locations, create new commands, and manipulate coordinates and text. Packed with tips on common coding errors.

The ABC's of Generic CADD
Alan R. Miller
278pp. Ref. 608-1

This outstanding guide to computer-aided design and drafting with Generic CADD assumes no previous experience with computers or CADD. This book will have users doing useful CADD work in record time, including basic drawing with the keyboard or a mouse, erasing and unerasing, making a copy of drawings on your printer, adding text and organizing your drawings using layers.

Advanced Techniques in AutoCAD (Second Edition)
Robert M. Thomas
425pp. Ref. 593-X

Develop custom applications using screen menus, command macros, and AutoLISP programming—no prior programming experience required. Topics include customizing the AutoCAD environment, advanced data extraction techniques, and much more.

AutoCAD Desktop Companion
SYBEX Ready Reference Series
Robert M. Thomas
1094pp. Ref. 590-5

This is a complete reference work covering all the features, commands, and user options available under AutoCAD Release 10, including drawing basic and complex entities, editing, displaying, printing, plotting, and customizing drawings, manipulating the drawing database, and AutoLISP programming. Through Release 10.

Mastering AutoCAD Release 11
George Omura
1150pp. Ref. 716-9

Even if you're just beginning, this comprehensive guide will help you to become an AutoCAD expert. Create your first drawing, then learn to use dimensions, enter pre-existing drawings, use advanced 3-D features, and more. Suitable for experienced users, too—includes tips and tricks you won't find elsewhere.

Mastering VersaCAD
David Bassett-Parkins
450pp. Ref. 617-0

For every level of VCAD user, this comprehensive tutorial treats each phase of project design including drawing, modifying, grouping, and filing. The reader will also learn VCAD project management and many tips, tricks, and shortcuts. Version 5.4.

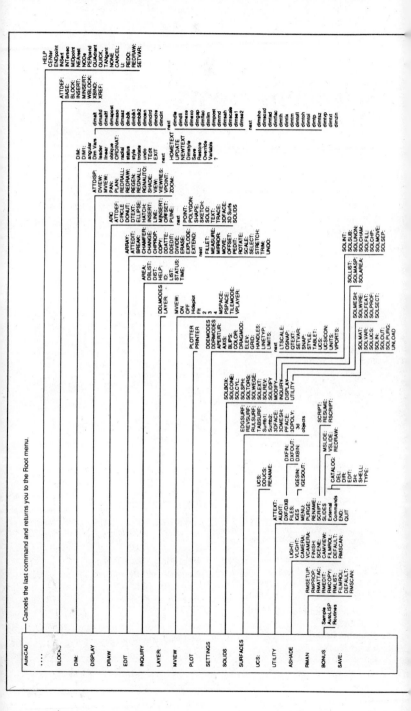